Contents

How to Do Well in Your Exam

A Your Speaking Test

This book is all about helping you to do well in the role-play part of your GCSE Speaking Test. In the test, this is what will happen:

- If you are entered for **Foundation Tier**, your test will last 8–10 minutes.
- If you are entered for **Higher Tier**, your test will last 10–12 minutes.
- You will begin with **two role-plays**, then you will give a **short presentation** which you have prepared in advance. Finally, you will have a **conversation** with your teacher.
- Your own French teacher will carry out the Test, which will be tape recorded.
- Your role-plays are worth one-third of the marks for the Speaking and are therefore very important.
- You have about 10 minutes to prepare before your test, with your two role-play cards. It is a good idea to give yourself about eight minutes to prepare the role-plays and leave about two minutes to think about your presentation.

B What you need to learn

- The syllabus for your exam is based on various topics. In this book, you can learn all the French you need to talk about these topics.
- You can enter the exam at Foundation Tier or at Higher Tier.
- If you are entered at Foundation Tier, you need only learn and practise the language and tasks for Foundation Tier and Foundation/Higher Tier, for each topic.
- If you are entered at Higher Tier, you must learn and practise all the language and tasks for every topic: this means that you need to work on all the pages of this book.

C How this book works

- This book is arranged in topics, the same as your exam syllabus.
- Each topic is divided into two parts:
  – Foundation Tier and Foundation/Higher Tier
  – Higher Tier
- Each part of each topic begins with a list of the key phrases you need to learn: see **D** below for some ideas about how to learn them.
- Beneath each list there is a cartoon: these cartoons help you to prepare for the conversations you may have in your test, using the phrases in the list.
- On the opposite page, you will find advice on how to prepare your role-plays and how to earn good marks. There are also practice role-plays which you can use to become really expert.

- On page 6, there is a list of important phrases which you can adapt to use in many topics.
- On page 7, you will find the French alphabet and advice on how to say all the letters. You must learn this really well as you will often be asked to spell something in your role-plays. This page also contains question words.
- On pages 70 to 75, you will find some role-play tests which have been set in the exam: you can use these to revise everything you have learnt in this book and to prepare for your Speaking Test.
- Page 76 contains French numbers, and the days and months in French.
- On pages 77 to 80, there is a glossary of words you may need while working on this book, French to English and English to French.

D How you can learn the key phrases

- The main thing when trying to learn is to use your brain to **do** things which will help you to understand and remember these key phrases.
- The lists are divided into small sections: work on one section at a time and master these phrases before moving on to the next section.
- It is easier and quicker in the end to learn the phrases really well: if you only half learn them, you will soon forget them.
- Work in sessions of 15 to 20 minutes, with a gap between sessions. So, if you have a learning homework of 45 minutes, it is best to do 15 minutes, then take a break (do another subject, for example), 15 more minutes followed by another break (listening to some music, for example) and then a final session of 15 minutes.
- In each learning session, use two or three different learning activities. Here are some you can use:

1 Look at a phrase you are trying to learn and say it several times in your head. Then close your eyes and say it five more times. Finally, open your eyes and check that you were right.

2 Keep a piece of paper in this book, just less than the size of the page. Cut out a section in the top right hand corner: it should be half of the page and about 4 cm deep, as shown:

I play football.

a When you are starting to get to know the phrases in a section, cover the English, look at the French and check that you can say the English for each phrase.

b Then cover the French and say or write all the French phrases to match the English.

c Gradually reveal the French phrases and see how quickly you can say what they are.

• You can do this from the top, e.g.

Je fais maths et français

• You can do it from the bottom, e.g.

Tu aimes la géographie?

• And you can do it from the side, e.g.

J'aime l'ang

d You can also cut a hole the size of a 10 pence coin in the middle of the piece of paper and move the hole around. You try to complete all the phrases that you see a part of, e.g.

3 Find ways to make the phrases your own, e.g.

a Change them to say what **you** want to say. If the phrase is *Ma matière préférée, c'est les maths*, change it to say what **your** favourite subject is.

b Find all the questions in the list and think who you would put them to: imagine yourself asking these people these questions. You may remember them better if you sometimes choose some silly people to put your questions to!

c Make up conversations in your head, using the phrases and adapting them: write some of them down.

4 It often helps to work with a partner and it is especially useful to test each other to be sure that you really know the phrases, e.g.

a Partner A thinks of two phrases in the list. Partner B says six of the phrases and scores five points every time he/she says one of Partner A's phrases.

b Partner A reads all the questions in the list and Partner B answers them without looking at the list.

c Partner A asks Partner B to spell some key words, e.g. *Anglais, ça s'écrit comment?*

d Partner A says a key word (as in the Higher Tier role-play cues) and Partner B says from memory a matching phrase from the list, e.g.

Partner A: *Nom.*

Partner B: *Je m'appelle Jessica.*

Partner A: *Anniversaire.*

Partner B: *Mon anniversaire, c'est le onze décembre.*

5 A really good way to learn is to write some notes for all the phrases in a section. Then try to "photograph" the phrases in your mind. Cover up the phrases and use your notes to help you to write the phrases in full. Below are some ways of making these notes:

a Write the sentences and omit all the vowels, e.g. *J'habite à Manchester. – J'hbt Mnchstr.*

b Write the first letter only of each word, e.g. *C'est une grande ville. – C'... u... g... v... .*

c Write the first and last words of each phrase, e.g. *La région est jolie. – La ... ... jolie.*

It will help you a lot if you gradually increase the time gap between covering up the phrases and writing them. Start off with a gap of five minutes, then gradually increase the gap to 15 minutes, an hour, a day, a week. Keeping them in your mind for longer and longer periods will help them to stay there permanently.

6 Begin each learning session by quickly testing yourself on what you learnt in the last session. Find an activity which you used in the previous session and see if you can still do it, e.g. cover the French phrases and say or write them from memory, looking at the English equivalents.

7 Before you start on a new topic, always revise one or two topics you learnt some time ago. This will help you to remember them for your exam and should also give you a pleasant surprise when you find that you still know them!

Exam Tip
The most important thing is to learn the key language really well. Then you will be able to use it correctly in your exam, and not only in the role-plays. The language you learn in this book will also help you to do well in your Conversation and in your Writing Test. Just follow this advice as you work through the book and you should enjoy your role-playing and do really well in your exam.

Useful Phrases

Bonjour	Hello
J'aime …	I like …
Je n'aime pas …	I don't like …
Tu veux … ?	Do you want … ? (to a friend)
Vous voulez … ?	Do you want … ? (to anyone else)
Je voudrais …	I'd like …
Tu aimes … ?	Do you like … ?
Je préfère …	I prefer …
Tu peux … ?	Can you … ? (to a friend)
Vous pouvez … ?	Can you … ? (to anyone else)
On peut … ?	Is it possible … ?
Pourquoi?	Why?
Parce que	Because
S'il te plaît	Please (to a friend)
S'il vous plaît	Please (to anyone else)
Y a-t-il … ?	Is there … ? Are there … ?
Il y a …	There is … There are …
Où est … ?	Where is … ?
Où sont … ?	Where are … ?
Tu as … ?	Have you got … ? (to a friend)
Vous avez … ?	Have you got … ? (to anyone else)
J'ai …	I have …
Je n'ai pas …	I haven't got …
Nous avons …	We've got …
Il/Elle a …	He/She/It has …

Qu'est-ce que … ?	What … ?
Qu'est-ce que c'est?	What is it?
Qu'est-ce que vous avez?	What have you got?
Je suis …	I am …
Il/Elle est …	He/She/It is …
C'était …	It was …
Je vais …	I'm going …
On va …	We're going …
Je m'excuse.	I'm sorry.
A mon avis	In my opinion
Par exemple	For example
Et	And
Mais	But
Il faut …	It is necessary …
D'habitude	Usually
Souvent	Often
Toujours	Always
Hier	Yesterday
La semaine dernière	Last week
Le week-end dernier	Last weekend
Demain	Tomorrow
Samedi prochain	Next Saturday
C'est combien?	How much is it?
Oui	Yes
Non	No
Merci (beaucoup)	Thank you (very much)
Au revoir	Goodbye

The Alphabet

> **Exam Tip**
> You must learn how to say the letters of the alphabet in French. You will often be asked to spell your name or where you live. Practise these before your exam.

Ça s'écrit comment?   How do you spell that?

A said like *a* in *cat*	**N** said like *enn*
B said like *bay*	**O** said like *o* in *only*
C said like *say*	**P** said like *pay*
D said like *day*	**Q** said like *coo*
E said like *e* in *the*	**R** said like *air*
F said like *eff*	**S** said like *ess*
G said like *shay*	**T** said like *tay*
H said like *ash*	**U** said like *u* in *cupid*
I said like *ee* in *meet*	**V** said like *vay*
J said like *she*	**W** said like *double vay*
K said like *ca* in *cat*	**X** said like *eeks*
L said like *ell*	**Y** said like *ee grec*
M said like *emm*	**Z** said like *zed*

Question Words

> **Exam Tip**
> - In your Speaking Test you will have to understand and answer your teacher's questions. You will not always be able to prepare in advance questions which are indicated by – ! –.
> - To do well in your exam, you must be able to answer questions quickly. To do this, you must know the question words really well.

Que?
Que fais-tu, le week-end?
What?
What do you do at the weekend?

Comment?
Comment viens-tu au collège?
How?
How do you come to school?

Où?
On se voit où?
Where?
Where shall we meet?

Quand?
Quand partez-vous?
When?
When are you leaving?

Quel / Quelle?
Le train part de quel quai?
Which?
Which platform does the train leave from?

Qui?
Avec qui vas-tu en vacances?
Who?
Who are you going on holiday with?

Combien?
C'est combien?
Vous êtes combien?
How much? How many?
How much is it?
How many of you are there?

Pourquoi?
Pourquoi aimes-tu l'anglais?
Why?
Why do you like English?

A quelle heure?
Le petit déjeuner est à quelle heure?
At what time?
At what time is breakfast?

Depuis quand?
Ça fait mal depuis quand?
Since when?
Since when has it been hurting?

Qu'est-ce qui?
Qu'est-ce qui ne va pas?
What?
What is wrong?

Qu'est-ce que?
Qu'est-ce que vous avez comme glaces?
What?
What sorts of ice creams have you got?

Pour parler des matières …

Je fais maths, français, informatique …
Quelle est ta matière préférée?
Ma matière préférée, c'est l'EMT (les maths).
Tu aimes la géographie (l'espagnol)?
J'aime l'anglais parce que c'est intéressant (utile).
Je suis fort(e) en histoire.
Je n'aime pas les sciences (l'EPS). C'est ennuyeux (difficile).
L'année prochaine, je voudrais faire allemand.

To talk about school subjects …

I'm doing maths, French, IT …
What's your favourite subject?
My favourite subject is technology (maths).
Do you like geography (Spanish)?
I like English because it's interesting (useful).
I'm good at history.
I don't like science (sport). It's boring (difficult).
Next year I'd like to do German.

Pour parler de votre journée …

Tu as combien de cours par jour?
On a cinq ou six cours par jour.
Normalement, les cours durent cinquante minutes.
Le premier cours commence à neuf heures et quart.
Les cours finissent à trois heures et demie.
A mon avis, c'est trop long (ce n'est pas trop long).
Le déjeuner est à midi dix. D'habitude, je mange à la cantine.

To talk about your day …

How many lessons a day do you have?
We have five or six lessons a day.
Normally, lessons last 50 minutes.
The first lesson starts at 9.15.
Lessons end at 3.30.
In my opinion, it's too long (it's not too long).
Lunch is at ten past twelve. Usually, I eat in the canteen.

Pour parler du collège …

Comment viens-tu au collège?
Normalement, je viens à pied (à vélo, en autobus).
Que penses-tu du collège?
Il est bien (affreux). Les profs sont gentils.
Il est grand (petit, moderne).
On s'amuse bien pendant la récréation.

To talk about school …

How do you come to school?
Normally, I come on foot (by bike, by bus).
What do you think of school?
It's OK (awful). The teachers are nice.
It's big (small, modern).
We enjoy ourselves during break.

Et le soir …

Le lundi, il y a un club d'informatique (de musique, dessin).
Je bavarde avec mes copains.
Nous jouons au football dans la cour. On va en ville.
Je fais deux heures de devoirs par soir.

And in the evening …

On Mondays, there is a computer (music, art) club.
I chat with my friends.
We play soccer in the playground. We go into town.
I do two hours of homework every evening.

Votre ami français vous pose des questions sur votre collège.

1 Write out the complete conversation.
2 Work with a partner. Partner A asks the questions and partner B answers them. Then swap roles.

Exam Practice

F **A**

1 Read these instructions. Then write the phrases on the right in the correct order to make the dialogue.

You are talking to your French friend about school.

- You normally come to school by bike.
- Your favourite subject is English.
- Ask if your friend likes IT.
- There is a computer club on Tuesdays.

2 Learn the dialogue. Then, looking only at the English instructions, practise it with a partner.

– Ah, c'est intéressant, ça!

– Ma matière préférée, c'est l'anglais.

– Comment viens-tu au collège?

– Tu aimes l'informatique?

– Quelle est ta matière préférée?

– Oui, parce que c'est utile et intéressant.

– Normalement, je viens en vélo.

– Le mardi, il y a un club d'informatique.

Exam Tip

In your exam, you will always have to ask a question. The instruction will begin like this:
- Ask if ...   • Ask what ...   • Ask when ...

Practise asking questions by matching these instructions and questions. Take turns to ask and answer the questions with your partner.

1 Ask if your friend does German.

2 Ask what your friend's favourite subject is.

3 Ask if your friend likes maths.

4 Ask how many lessons your friend has each day.

a Tu aimes les maths?

b Quelle est ta matière préférée?

c Tu fais allemand?

d Tu as combien de cours par jour?

F **B**

1 Cover the Teacher's Role and prepare your part.

2 Uncover the Teacher's Role and practise the dialogue with a partner. Write it in full and learn it.

Exam Tip

When the instructions say that your teacher will play the part of your friend, remember to use *tu* not *vous*, e.g.

Tu aimes ...   Quelle est **ta** matière préférée?

(Adapted from AQA/NEAB – 1998)

Teacher's Role	Candidate's Role
Tu es chez ton ami(e) en France. Moi, je suis ton ami(e). 1 Quelle est ta matière préférée? 2 Pourquoi? 3 Je comprends. 4 Pas trop. C'est difficile. 5 Bonne chance!	You are talking to your French friend about school. 1 Say you prefer English. 2 Say the teacher is interesting. 3 Ask if your friend likes maths. 4 Say you want to do geography and English next year. Your teacher will play the part of your friend and will speak first.

 C

1 Cover the Teacher's Role. Look at the **!** in the Candidate's Role and think what questions your teacher could ask. Write a list, then answer each one.

2 Uncover the Teacher's Role. Did you include the teacher's third question?

3 Work with a partner to practise each part.

Exam Tip

In your Foundation/Higher Tier role-play, you will always see a **!**. This means that your teacher will ask you a question. In your preparation time, try to work out what this question might be.

Teacher's Role	Candidate's Role
Tu es chez ton ami(e) en France. Moi, je suis ton ami(e). 1 Normalement, comment viens-tu au collège? 2 Les cours durent combien de temps? 3 Les cours finissent à quelle heure? 4 Tu fais combien de devoirs, le soir? The teacher plays the part of the friend and speaks first.	You are talking to your French friend about your school day. 1 Tell him/her how you get to school. 2 Tell him/her how long your lessons last. 3 **!** 4 Tell him/her how much homework you do each evening.

9

Depuis combien de temps …

Tu apprends le français (le russe) depuis combien de temps?

J'apprends l'allemand (la religion) depuis trois ans.

Vous connaissez d'autres langues étrangères?

Je parle couramment l'urdu. J'aimerais apprendre le portugais.

For how long …

For how long have you been learning French (Russian)?

I've been learning German (religion) for three years.

Do you know any other foreign languages?

I speak Urdu fluently. I'd like to learn Portuguese.

Pour parler de votre emploi du temps …

Qu'est-ce que vous avez, le jeudi?

Le mercredi, j'ai espagnol et chimie le matin, et musique et italien l'après-midi.

Moi, je trouve que les récréations ne sont pas assez longues.

Les vacances de Noël (de Pâques, d'été) sont trop courtes.

Le trimestre prochain commence (finit) le premier septembre (le vingt décembre).

A mon avis, nous faisons trop de matières.

Les sciences ne devraient pas être obligatoires.

Qu'en penses-tu?

Je suis d'accord avec toi.

To talk about your timetable …

What do you have on Thursdays?

On Wednesdays, I have Spanish and chemistry in the morning, and music and Italian in the afternoon.

I find that the breaks are not long enough.

The Christmas (Easter, summer) holidays are too short.

Next term starts (finishes) on the 1st of September (the 20th of December).

In my opinion, we do too many subjects.

Science should not be compulsory.

What do you think about it?

I agree with you.

Pour dire si vous êtes pour ou contre …

Tu dois porter un uniforme au collège?

Oui, les garçons doivent porter un pantalon gris, une chemise blanche et une veste bleue.

Tu peux me décrire ton uniforme scolaire?

Les filles portent une jupe noire, un chemisier blanc et un pull-over rouge.

Que penses-tu de l'uniforme obligatoire?

Je suis pour, parce que c'est pratique et pas cher.

Je suis contre, parce que c'est laid et cher.

La plupart des règles scolaires sont bien.

Mais il y a des règles bêtes.

Par exemple, on devrait pouvoir rester en classe quand il pleut.

To say if you are for or against …

Do you have to wear a uniform at school?

Yes, the boys have to wear grey trousers, a white shirt and a blue jacket.

Can you describe your school uniform for me?

The girls wear a black skirt, a white blouse and a red pullover.

What do you think about compulsory uniform?

I'm for it, because it's convenient and not expensive.

I'm against it, because it's ugly and expensive.

Most of the school rules are fine.

But there are some stupid rules.

For example, we should be able to stay in class when it rains.

Votre amie française fait une enquête et vous pose des questions.
Complétez ces réponses.

1 Write your answers by completing the sentences.

2 Then work with a partner: take turns to ask and answer these questions.

Exam Practice

A

1 Give yourself four minutes to prepare the role-play on the right, without using a dictionary.

2 When you see this – **!** – you will have to respond to something which you have not prepared. However, you can try to anticipate what your teacher will ask you and prepare some good replies. You can use a 'mind map' to do this, as in the example below.

You are talking with a French friend about your school.
- Langues.
- Uniforme.
- Règles scolaires.
- **!**

Exam Tip
Will you use *tu* or *vous* when you talk to your teacher? Why?

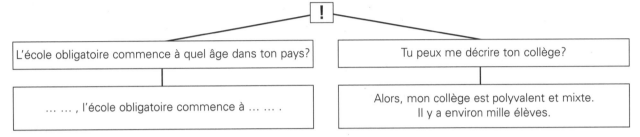

| ! |
| L'école obligatoire commence à quel âge dans ton pays? | Tu peux me décrire ton collège? |
| ... ... , l'école obligatoire commence à ... . | Alors, mon collège est polyvalent et mixte. Il y a environ mille élèves. |

3 Now study the dialogue below and try to complete and then learn your answers.

4 Practise with a partner: one of you reads the teacher's questions and the other listens (without looking at the text) and answers. To practise coping with the unexpected, change the teacher's last question, using one you prepared above.

Professeur: Tu apprends quelles langues étrangères?

Vous: ... le français et l'espagnol.

Professeur: Tu les apprends depuis combien de temps?

Vous: Alors, ... le français depuis ... ... et l'espagnol ... ...

Professeur: Tu dois porter un uniforme au collège?

Vous: Oui, c'est obligatoire. Les garçons ... porter un pantalon ..., une chemise ... et ... ... Pour les filles, c'est la même chose, mais elles peuvent ... une jupe ... .

Professeur: Que penses-tu, en général, des règles scolaires?

Vous: A mon ..., la ... des règles sont ... . Mais je ... qu'il y a des règles ... .

Professeur: Tu peux me donner un exemple d'une règle que tu trouves bête?

Vous: Oui, on devrait ... rester en ... quand il ... .

Professeur: Merci.

B

1 Revise pages 8 and 10 and make sure you know all the key sentences.

2 Cover the Teacher's Role and give yourself just four minutes to prepare this role-play. Remember how to prepare to respond to the **!** .

Teacher's Role	**Candidate's Role**
1 Quelle est ton opinion sur les récréations et que fais-tu pendant les récréations? 2 Tu peux me décrire ton uniforme scolaire et me dire ce que tu en penses? 3 Quelles langues apprends-tu, au collège, et depuis quand? 4 Merci.	You are talking about school with a friend from Belgium. 1 Récréations. 2 Uniforme. 3 Description. 4 ! Your teacher will play the part of your friend and will speak first.

3 Now work with a partner and help each other to make up the best answers you can think of.

4 Practise the role-play until you can both perform it perfectly. Sometimes, change the teacher's last question to practise responding to something unexpected.

Pour aider à la maison …

Que fais-tu pour aider à la maison?
Je mets la table tous les jours. Je prépare aussi le petit déjeuner.
Hier, j'ai nettoyé ma chambre.
Le week-end prochain, je vais faire le jardinage avec mon père.
Je fais mon lit (les courses, la vaisselle) de temps en temps.

Tu aimes faire le ménage? Ah non, c'est trop dur!
Je n'aime pas passer l'aspirateur (laver la voiture).

Pour parler de là où vous habitez …

Où habites-tu? Mon adresse, c'est le cent deux, rue de l'Ecole.
J'habite un petit appartement dans un grand immeuble.
J'habite une maison moderne. Nous avons un garage et un jardin.
On est assez près du (loin du) centre-ville.
J'habite un village vieux et typique.
Nous sommes dans la banlieue.
J'aime notre maison. Elle n'est pas trop grande.

Pour décrire votre maison …

Comment est ta maison?
Nous avons deux (trois) chambres.
Dans la cuisine, il y a un frigo et une cuisinière.
La salle de bains est en haut, en face de ma chambre.
Nous n'avons pas de lave-vaisselle.
La télévision (la chaîne hi-fi) est au salon.
Dans ma chambre, il y a une armoire, une table et une chaise.
Les murs sont blancs et rouges. Les rideaux sont bleus.
Je partage ma chambre avec mon frère (ma sœur).
Que fais-tu dans ta chambre?
Je dors, je fais mes devoirs et je regarde la télé.

To help at home …

What do you do to help at home?
I set the table every day. I also prepare breakfast.
Yesterday, I cleaned my room.
Next weekend, I'm going to do the gardening with my dad.
I make my bed (do the shopping, do the washing up) from time to time.
Do you like doing housework? Oh no, it's too hard!
I don't like doing the hoovering (washing the car).

To talk about where you live …

Where do you live? My address is 102, School Street.
I live in a small flat in a big block of flats.
I live in a modern house. We have a garage and a garden.
We're quite near to (a long way from) the town centre.
I live in an old and typical village.
We're in the suburbs.
I like our house. It's not too big.

To describe your home …

What's your house like?
We have two (three) bedrooms.
In the kitchen, there is a fridge and a cooker.
The bathroom is upstairs, opposite my bedroom.
We haven't got a dishwasher.
The television (hi-fi system) is in the living room.
In my room, there is a wardrobe, a table and a chair.
The walls are white and red. The curtains are blue.
I share my room with my brother (my sister).
What do you do in your bedroom?
I sleep, I do my homework and I watch TV.

Vous allez à une surprise-partie et vous faites la connaissance d'un(e) jeune français(e).

1 The answers are printed as one long word. Write them out correctly.
2 Work with a partner to practise the conversation, then learn it.
3 Partner A takes the part of the boy and reads his questions. Partner B closes the book and answers the questions. Then swap roles.

Exam Practice

 A

1 Cover the dialogue on the right and prepare this role-play in four minutes.

You are staying with a friend in Quebec. You are talking about what you do at home.

- You do the washing up from time to time.
- You also do the gardening.
- Ask if your friend does the housework.
- You think housework is very hard.

2 Write the dialogue in full, then practise it with a partner until you are both word perfect.

Tu es chez ton ami(e) au Québec. Moi, je suis ton ami(e).

– Qu'est-ce que tu fais pour aider à la maison?

– **Je de temps en temps.**

– C'est tout?

– **Non, je fais aussi **

– Alors moi non, je déteste ça.

– **Tu ⌐ ?**

– Oui, parfois. Tu aimes faire le ménage?

– **Non, c'est très 🧹**

B

1 Revise all the phrases on page 12. Ask your partner to test you.

2 Cover the Model Dialogue and prepare the role-play in four minutes.

3 Look at the Model Dialogue and practise with a partner until you are both perfect.

Candidate's Role

You are staying with a French friend in France. You are talking about what you do at home.
1 You make your bed.
2 You prepare breakfast.
3 Ask if your French friend likes doing the gardening.
4 You think housework is boring.

Your teacher will play the part of your friend and will speak first.

Model Dialogue

– Qu'est-ce que tu fais pour aider à la maison?

– **Je fais mon lit.**

– C'est tout?

– **Je prépare aussi le petit déjeuner.**

– Moi aussi.

– **Tu aimes faire le jardinage?**

– Ah non! Je déteste ça. Tu aimes faire le ménage?

– **Non, c'est ennuyeux.**

– Tu n'es pas le seul (la seule).

(Adapted from AQA/NEAB – 1998)

C

1 Cover the Teacher's Role below. Think what questions your teacher could ask for the **!** . Write a list, then write a good answer to each question.

2 Uncover the Teacher's Role. Did you have the last question in your list?

3 Act the dialogue with a partner.

4 Write out the conversation and learn it by heart.

Exam Tips

- As you prepare, work out what the **!** question might be and how you might answer it. Always listen carefully when your teacher asks this question. If you need time to think, you can say *Alors, eh bien …* while you think.

- When you answer a question, try always to give two pieces of information. This is made clear in the instructions. But you should also try to do this in answer to **!** , where it is not made clear.

Teacher's Role

Tu parles avec ton ami(e) français(e). Moi, je suis ton ami(e).
1 Où habites-tu?
2 Comment est ta maison?
3 Que fais-tu pour aider à la maison?
4 Moi aussi. Et qu'est-ce que tu n'aimes pas faire pour aider à la maison?

Candidate's Role

Your French friend asks about where you live.
1 Tell your friend that you live near the town centre.
2 Say that your house is quite big, with four bedrooms.
3 Say that you set the table every day and do the shopping.
4 **!**

When you see this – **!** – you will have to respond to something which you have not prepared.
Your teacher will play the part of your friend and will speak first.

Home Life: Visiting

Quand vous voulez prendre un bain …
Je peux prendre un bain, s'il vous plaît?
Je voudrais prendre une douche.
Bien sûr.
Tu as besoin de quelque chose?
Oui, j'ai oublié ma serviette.
Oui, je m'excuse, mais je n'ai plus de dentifrice.
Ça ne fait rien. Je vais te donner du shampooing.
J'ai besoin d'une brosse à dents (de savon).
Merci beaucoup.

When you want to have a bath …
Please may I have a bath?
I'd like to have a shower.
Of course.
Do you need anything?
Yes, I've forgotten my towel.
Yes, I'm sorry but I've got no toothpaste left.
That doesn't matter. I'll give you some shampoo.
I need a toothbrush (some soap).
Thanks very much.

Quand vous cherchez une pièce …
Voilà ta chambre.
Où est le salon, s'il te plaît?
Il est par ici (par là).
Où se trouvent les toilettes?
La salle de séjour est en bas, à côté de la salle à manger.
Nous n'avons pas de cave.
Votre (Ta) maison est très jolie (grande).
Elle est assez petite.

When you are looking for a room …
This is your bedroom.
Where is the lounge, please?
It's this way (that way).
Where is the toilet?
The living room is downstairs, next to the dining room.
We haven't got a cellar.
Your house is very pretty (big).
It's quite small.

Pour parler des repas …
On mange à quelle heure, s'il te plaît?
On prend le petit déjeuner vers sept heures.
Le déjeuner est à midi.
Nous dînons vers six heures et demie.
Tu prends le goûter d'habitude?
Oui, j'aime beaucoup ça.
Tu as faim (soif)?
Tu manges à quelle heure, chez toi?

To talk about meals …
At what time do we eat, please?
We have breakfast at about 7 o'clock.
Lunch is at midday.
We have dinner at about 6.30.
Do you usually have an afternoon snack?
Yes, I like that very much.
Are you hungry (thirsty)?
At what time do you eat at home?

Vous allez passer quelques jours chez une amie française. Vous arrivez chez elle.

1 Only the top half of the words is printed. Write out all the questions and answers in full.

2 With a partner, practise reading the conversation aloud. Then learn it.

Exam Practice

 A

1 Revise all the phrases on pages 12 and 14. Ask a partner to test you.

2 Look at this table. Take a phrase from each box to make up a question, e.g. *Je peux prendre une douche, s'il te plaît?*

3 Write as many questions as you can, based on this table, in five minutes.

Je peux Tu as Où est Où se trouvent On mange Tu prends Tu manges	à quelle heure prendre une douche les toilettes le goûter besoin de prendre un bain ma chambre la salle de bains	d'habitude? s'il te plaît? chez toi? quelque chose? s'il vous plaît?

4 Now write a conversation using your questions and making up answers to them.

 B

1 Cover the Dialogue below and prepare your role.

2 Uncover the Dialogue and write it out in full, filling the gaps with the words in the box below.

3 Your partner covers the Dialogue: you play the teacher's part and your partner plays the candidate. Then change parts.

> **Exam Tip**
>
> In your exam, you will have about eight minutes to prepare two role-plays. Try to prepare this one in just three minutes. In your exam, the role-play with the higher number (7–12) will be at Foundation/Higher Tier. It is always harder and you will do better if you leave five minutes to prepare it.

Candidate's Role

You are staying with a friend in Switzerland.
1 Say you would like to have a shower.
2 You've forgotten your toothbrush and toothpaste.
3 Ask where the bathroom is.
4 Ask when lunch is.

Your teacher will play the part of your friend and will speak first.

Dialogue

– Tu … prendre un bain?

– **Je … prendre … … .**

– Bien sûr. Tu … besoin de quelque … ?

– **Oui, je m'excuse, mais … … ma … et mon … .**

– Ça ne … rien. Je … te donner une … et du … .

– **Merci … . … est la … … … ?**

– Elle … par ici, en face … ta chambre.

– **Le … est à quelle … , s'il te … ?**

plaît	veux	une douche	déjeuner	as	voudrais	est	heure	chose	beaucoup	j'ai
oublié	de	fait	dentifrice	où	brosse à dents	salle de bains	vais			

 C

1 Cover the Teacher's Role and give yourself five minutes to prepare.

2 Uncover the Teacher's Role and write the dialogue.

3 Work with a partner and take turns to play each part.

> **Exam Tips**
>
> • Will you use *tu* or *vous* when you speak? Why?
>
> • Anticipate the questions your teacher might ask at the ! and prepare some good answers: remember to give two details.

Teacher's Role

Tu arrives chez ton ami(e). Moi, je suis ton ami(e).
1 Alors, voilà ta chambre.
2 Bien sûr. Tu as besoin de quelque chose?
3 D'accord.
4 Merci beaucoup.
5 Oui, bien sûr. On va à la cuisine, si tu veux.

Candidate's Role

You have just arrived at your French friend's house.
1 Ask if you can please have a bath.
2 !
3 Tell your friend that his/her house is very pretty.
4 Say you are hungry and ask if your friend usually has an afternoon snack.

Your teacher will play the part of your friend and will speak first.

Pour parler des repas …

Chez nous, on prend le petit déjeuner vers sept heures d'habitude.
Je préfère manger plus tôt (plus tard).
Mon plat préféré, c'est le steak frites (la salade de tomates).
Je n'aime pas le cidre (la bière).
Chez nous, on mange beaucoup de poisson.
Et vous, qu'est-ce que vous aimez manger (boire)?
Je ne peux pas manger la viande (les œufs). Je suis végétarien(ne).
Je suis allergique aux noix (au lait).

To talk about meals …

At home, we usually have breakfast at about 7 o'clock.
I prefer to eat earlier (later).
My favourite dish is steak and chips (tomato salad).
I don't like cider (beer).
In our house, we eat a lot of fish.
And you, what do you like to eat (to drink)?
I can't eat meat (eggs). I'm vegetarian.
I'm allergic to nuts (to milk).

Quand vous faites le ménage …

Je peux vous aider?
Tu sais faire la lessive (repasser)?
Je pourrais nettoyer la baignoire (balayer la cuisine).
Tu peux m'aider?
Je ferai la vaisselle, si tu veux.

When you're doing the housework …

Can I help you?
Can you do the washing (iron)?
I could clean the bath (sweep the kitchen).
Can you help me?
I'll do the washing up, if you like.

Pour dire qui fait quoi …

Qui fait le ménage chez toi?
Mon père fait toujours la cuisine.
C'est moi qui fais la plupart du travail.
Mon frère s'occupe du jardin.
Ma mère n'aime pas faire les courses.
Ma sœur ne fait rien. Elle est paresseuse.
Ce n'est pas juste, à mon avis.

To say who does what …

Who does the housework in your house?
My father always does the cooking.
I'm the one who does most of the work.
My brother looks after the garden.
My mother doesn't like shopping.
My sister does nothing. She is lazy.
It's not fair, in my opinion.

Pour dire si vous partagez votre chambre …

Vous partagez votre (Tu partages ta) chambre?
Je partage ma chambre avec mon frère (ma sœur).
Je ne partage pas ma chambre.
Tu as de la chance!
Je voudrais bien avoir une chambre pour moi tout(e) seul(e).

To say if you share your room …

Do you share your room?
I share my room with my brother (my sister).
I don't share my room.
You're lucky!
I'd really like to have a room to myself.

Vous êtes chez une amie, en Belgique. Il est six heures et vous avez faim.

Imagine that the Belgian girl is visiting the British girl. Change the words underlined and
write the new conversation.

Exam Practice

A

1 Revise all the phrases on pages 12, 14 and 16, and prepare the role-play.

2 Then write the jumbled sentences on the right in the correct order to make the dialogue. Practise with a partner until you can both perform both parts perfectly.

You are visiting a friend in Paris and you are talking about life at home.

1 Plats préférés.   3 Qui fait quoi?
2 !   4 Votre chambre.

– Quels sont tes plats préférés?
– Qu'est-ce que tu n'aimes pas manger?
– Chez toi, qui fait quoi pour aider à la maison?
– Et tu as une chambre pour toi toute seule?
– Je n'aime ni la viande ni le poisson parce que je suis végétarienne.
– Non, je partage avec ma sœur.
– Alors, ma mère fait toujours la cuisine et moi je fais la vaisselle.

B

Exam Tip

In your exam, there are four marks for each task. To earn four marks, you need to communicate everything you are asked for, clearly and without any mistakes. You must listen carefully to your teacher's questions and give all the details asked for – usually **two** pieces of information for each task. Don't worry if you miss a piece of information, as your teacher will ask another question to give you a second chance. For example:
– Chez toi, on prend les repas à quelle heure?
– On prend le petit déjeuner vers sept heures.

The candidate should mention two meals, so the teacher then asks:
– Et les autres repas, on les prend à quelle heure?
– On prend le dîner à six heures et demie.
The candidate scores four marks but could have done it more easily by answering the first question fully, e.g.
– On prend le petit déjeuner vers sept heures et le dîner à six heures et demie.

1 Look at the Candidate's Role and prepare your part.

2 Then look at the dialogue on the right. Notice that the teacher has to ask extra questions. Try to give all the information the examiner requires by answering fully the questions underlined.

3 Write out the dialogue so that the candidate gives all the information required in just four answers. Then practise both parts with a partner.

Candidate's Role

You are staying with a friend in Sénégal and you are talking about life at home.
1 Repas.
2 Ménage.
3 Votre chambre.
4 !

– <u>Chez toi, on mange à quelle heure?</u>
– **Nous dînons vers six heures.**
– Et les autres repas?
– **On prend le petit déjeuner vers sept heures.**
– <u>Que fais-tu pour aider à la maison?</u>
– **Normalement, je fais les courses.**
– C'est tout?
– **Non, je fais la vaisselle aussi.**
– <u>Et tu dois partager ta chambre?</u>
– **Oui, je partage ma chambre.**
– Avec qui?
– **Je partage ma chambre avec ma petite sœur.**
– <u>Et comment trouves-tu cela?</u>
– **Je n'aime pas partager ma chambre avec ma sœur.**
– Pourquoi?
– **Parce que ce n'est pas juste, à mon avis.**

C

1 Cover the Teacher's Role and prepare this role-play in five minutes.

2 Practise with a partner. Help each other to score all 16 marks.

Teacher's Role

1 Chez toi, on prend les repas à quelle heure?
2 Qui fait le ménage, chez toi?
3 Qu'est-ce que tu ne sais pas faire?
4 Que penses-tu des familles où les femmes font tout le travail?

Candidate's Role

You are staying with a friend in Belgium and you are discussing meals and housework.
1 Repas.
2 Ménage.
3 !
4 Opinion.

Pour dire comment ça va …	To say how you are …
Comment vas-tu (allez-vous)?	How are you?
Comme ci, comme ça.	Not bad.
J'avais froid mais maintenant j'ai chaud.	I was cold but now I'm hot.
J'ai très soif (faim). Je suis assez fatigué(e).	I'm very thirsty (hungry). I'm quite tired.
Je me sens malade. Je peux me coucher?	I feel ill. Can I go to bed?
Tu te sens mieux?	Do you feel better?
Ça va bien, merci.	I'm fine, thanks.
Ça va mal. Ça va mieux.	Not very well. I'm feeling better.
Tu veux rester au lit?	Do you want to stay in bed?
Tu peux marcher?	Can you walk?

Pour dire ce qui ne va pas …	To say what's wrong …
Où est-ce que vous avez (tu as) mal?	Where does it hurt?
Qu'est-ce qui ne va pas?	What's wrong?
J'ai mal à la tête (aux dents).	I've got a headache (tooth ache).
J'ai mal au dos (à l'oreille, à la gorge).	My back (ear, throat) hurts.
Je suis tombé(e). Je me suis fait mal au genou (à la main).	I fell down. I hurt my knee (my hand).
Ça me fait mal quand je bouge. Ça fait mal ici (là).	It hurts when I move. It hurts here (there).
Je suis enrhumé(e).	I've got a cold.
Ça fait mal depuis quand?	How long has it been hurting?
J'ai mal au ventre depuis hier.	I've had stomach ache since yesterday.

Pour demander de l'aide …	To ask for help …
Au secours! Vous pouvez m'aider, s'il vous plaît?	Help! Can you help me, please?
Tu peux me donner un coup de main, s'il te plaît?	Can you give me a hand, please?
Vous avez de l'aspirine? Je peux avoir de l'eau?	Do you have any aspirin? May I have some water?
Je voudrais voir un médecin.	I'd like to see a doctor.

Ⓐ Vous êtes chez votre ami français. Un jour, vous vous sentez malade.

Ⓑ Vous jouez au football et vous vous êtes fait mal au genou.

1 Write the two conversations in full. Use these symbols to help you fill each gap.

2 Work with your partner, taking it in turns to ask and answer the questions.

18

Exam Practice

A

1 Revise the phrases on page 18 and ask your partner to test you.
2 Work on the role-play with a partner and take turns to play the candidate.
3 Write out the dialogue in full.
4 Write a different answer to each question, by changing one detail.
Example: *Je me sens **assez** fatigué(e).*

Teacher's Role	Candidate's Role
Tu es chez des amis en France et tu te sens malade après une longue promenade.	You're staying with friends in France and you don't feel very well after a long walk.
1 Comment vas–tu?	1 Say you feel very tired.
2 Tu es malade?	2 Say you are quite thirsty.
3 C'est tout?	3 Say that you have a headache.
4 Tu es tombé(e)?	4 Say that you have hurt your knee.
5 Tu as besoin de quelque chose?	5 Ask for some aspirin.
6 Qu'est-ce que tu veux faire?	6 Ask if you can go to bed.
7 Bien sûr. Et je vais te donner de l'aspirine et de l'eau.	Your teacher will play the part of your friend and will speak first.

B

1 Cover the Dialogue and prepare the role-play.
2 Complete the answers in the Dialogue.
3 Work with a partner to practise both parts.
4 Write the conversation in full and keep it for revision.

Exam Tips

• Prepare your first role-play in just three minutes. This leaves more time for the second one, which has more marks!
• Only use a dictionary if you really do not know a word you need, or you will waste time. If you must look up a word, make sure you pronounce it correctly or you will lose marks.

Candidate's Role	Dialogue
You wake up one morning feeling ill. Your French friend comes to see you.	– Comment vas-tu?
1 Say you feel ill.	– **Je me sens … .**
2 Say that you have a stomach ache.	– Où as-tu mal?
3 Ask if you can stay in bed.	– **J'ai … au ventre.**
4 Ask for some aspirin.	– Qu'est-ce que tu veux faire?
	– **Je … rester au lit?**
	– Oui, bien sûr. Tu as besoin de quelque chose?
	– **Je peux … de l'aspirine, s'il te plaît?**

C

1 Cover the Teacher's Role and prepare your part.
2 Now look at the Teacher's Role. Did you guess the question?
3 Write out the completed role-play.
4 Work with a partner to get good answers. Then practise until you can both produce the candidate's part without the book.

Teacher's Role	Candidate's Role
Tu es chez ton ami(e) français(e). Moi, je suis le père (la mère) de ton ami(e).	You don't feel well and you talk to your French friend's parent about it.
1 Comment vas-tu?	1 Say that you feel ill.
2 Où est-ce que tu as mal?	2 Your head aches and you have a stomach ache.
3 Tu te sens malade depuis quand?	3 !
4 Que veux-tu faire?	4 Say you would like to see a doctor.
5 D'accord, je vais l'appeler.	

Quand vous voulez aller voir un médecin, un dentiste ou un pharmacien …
Vous avez l'air malade.
J'ai mal aux dents depuis deux jours.
A mon avis, je devrais aller voir un dentiste. Je vais l'appeler.
Je pourrais venir voir le médecin, s'il vous plaît?
Quand voulez-vous venir?
Je voudrais le voir aujourd'hui (cet après-midi).
Il est libre ce matin?
Vous pourriez venir demain, à onze heures? C'est urgent?

When you want to go and see a doctor, a dentist or a chemist …
You look ill.
I've had toothache for two days.
In my opinion, I should go and see a dentist. I'll call him.
Could I come and see the doctor, please?
When would you like to come?
I'd like to see him today (this afternoon).
Is he free this morning?
Could you come tomorrow, at 11 o'clock? Is it urgent?

Pour répondre aux questions …
Vous souffrez depuis combien de temps?
J'ai de la fièvre depuis avant-hier.
Vous avez la grippe.
Qu'est-ce qui s'est passé?
J'ai eu un accident. Je me suis cassé la jambe.
Je me suis brûlé le doigt. Je me suis coupé le pied.
Vous avez passé trop de temps au soleil et vous avez une insolation.
Je vais vous donner une ordonnance tout de suite.
Je vous conseille d'aller à la pharmacie.
Voilà un médicament.
C'est assez grave. Je dois contacter quelqu'un.
Vous pouvez téléphoner à mes parents. Voici leur numéro: c'est le …

To answer questions …
For how long have you been ill?
I've had a temperature since the day before yesterday.
You have flu.
What's happened?
I've had an accident. I've broken my leg.
I've burnt my finger. I've cut my foot.
You've spent too long in the sun and you've got sunstroke.
I'll give you a prescription straight away.
I advise you to go to the chemist's.
Here is a medicine.
It's quite serious. I must contact someone.
You can phone my parents. Here is their number: it's …

Pour parler d'une vie saine …
Que fais-tu (faites-vous) pour être en forme?
Il faut pratiquer un sport. Je suis un régime équilibré.
Il vaut mieux manger beaucoup de fruits et de légumes.
Je me couche de bonne heure toute la semaine.

To talk about a healthy life …
What do you do to stay fit?
It's necessary to practise a sport. I keep to a balanced diet.
It's best to eat a lot of fruit and vegetables.
I go to bed early all week.

Vous êtes chez votre ami en France et vous vous sentez malade.

1 Read this story and learn the lines of the boy who is ill.
2 Cover the story. Your partner reads the lines of the other people. You use these cues to help you play the sick boy's part:
   • Stomach ache. • Phone doctor. • Appointment. • Fish … diarrhoea. • Serious? • Go to bed.

Exam Practice

A

1 Read the two gapped dialogues below.

2 Choose the best answer for each gap from those in the box.

3 Practise the completed dialogues with your partner.

4 Partner B reads the questions. Partner A closes the book and makes up a new answer to each question. Then change roles.

Dialogue 1

– Je pourrais venir voir le dentiste, s'il vous plaît?

– ....

– Oui, j'ai vraiment très mal depuis trois jours. Je peux venir cet après-midi?

– ....

– Je suis tombé(e) et je me suis cassé une dent. Vous pouvez m'aider?

– ....

– Ça fait toujours mal. Vous pourriez me donner de l'aspirine?

– ....

Dialogue 2

– Mais dis donc, tu as l'air vraiment bien! Que fais-tu pour être en forme?

– ....

– Alors, que faut-il manger, à ton avis?

– ....

– Et, à ton avis, que faut-il faire aussi pour avoir une vie saine?

– ....

– Est-ce que tu fumes?

– ....

---

a Oui, venez à quinze heures trente. Le dentiste vous verra.

b C'est urgent?

c Non, à mon avis, il est essential d'éviter le tabac et l'alcool.

d Alors, je suis un régime équilibré.

e Non, mais je vais vous donner une ordonnance et je vous conseille d'aller à la pharmacie.

f Oui, je vais soigner votre dent. Ce n'est pas grave.

g Je pense qu'il vaut mieux manger beaucoup de légumes et de poisson.

h Il faut pratiquer un sport, comme le tennis, par exemple.

B

1 Revise the phrases on pages 18 and 20. Ask your partner to test you.

2 Cover the Teacher's Role and Model Dialogue and prepare your part.

3 Look at the Teacher's Role and write out the complete role-play.

4 Look at the Model Dialogue and compare it with your answer.

5 Practise the dialogue with your partner.

Exam Tips

- Will you say *vous* or *tu* to your teacher in this role? Why?
- Remember to give all the information the teacher asks for and to give two pieces of information whenever you can.

Teacher's Role

1 Alors, qu'est-ce qui ne va pas?
   (Candidate's task: to describe his/her symptoms.)
2 Et qu'est-ce qui s'est passé?
   (Candidate's task: to say he/she has had an accident.)
3 Ça s'est passé où et quand?
   (Candidate's task: to say where and when it happened.)
4 Je dois contacter quelqu'un. Qui pourrais-je contacter?
   (Candidate's task: to say who can be contacted and give a telephone number.)

Candidate's Role

You have had an accident while in France and go to the hospital.
1 Symptômes.
2 Accident.
3 Où et quand.
4 !

Your teacher will play the part of the doctor and will speak first.

(AQA/NEAB – 1998)

Model Dialogue

– Alors, qu'est-ce qui ne va pas?

– **Je pense que je me suis cassé la jambe et j'ai très mal à la tête.**

– Et qu'est-ce qui s'est passé?

– **J'ai eu un accident.**

– Ça s'est passé où et quand?

– **Je suis tombé(e) dans la rue ce matin, à dix heures.**

– Je dois contacter quelqu'un. Qui pourrais-je contacter?

– **Vous pouvez téléphoner à mes parents. Voici leur numéro: c'est le 00 44 ...**

Pour dire ce que vous aimez manger et boire …
Tu aimes la soupe de tomates (les côtelettes de porc)?
J'aime bien le café (le jus d'orange).
Je n'aime pas beaucoup les omelettes.
Le repas était très bon.
Je n'ai pas aimé l'entrecôte (les haricots verts). C'était trop froid.

Quand vous êtes à table …
Tu veux un peu de gâteau (confiture)?
Merci, ça va bien comme ça.
C'était délicieux, mais j'ai assez bu (mangé).
Encore du thé (de la limonade)?
Oui, avec plaisir, j'aime beaucoup le fromage (les fraises).
Passe-moi le pain (le sel), s'il te plaît.

Pour parler avec le serveur (la serveuse) …
Monsieur (Madame), s'il vous plaît.
Vous avez choisi?
Je prends le menu à cent vingt francs.
Pour commencer, les crudités.
Ensuite je voudrais le poulet frites.
Comme dessert, je prendrai une crêpe (une pêche).
Nous prenons un sandwich au jambon (au pâté).
Et comme boisson?
Donnez-nous une bouteille d'eau minérale, s'il vous plaît.
Vous avez de la moutarde (de l'huile), s'il vous plaît?

Pour demander quelque chose …
Qu'est-ce que vous avez comme glaces (yaourts)?
Nous avons vanille, chocolat et framboise.
Le plat du jour, qu'est-ce que c'est exactement?

Après le repas …
L'addition, s'il vous plaît.
Pardon, où se trouve le téléphone?
Au sous-sol, à côté des toilettes.

To say what you like to eat and drink …
Do you like tomato soup (pork chops)?
I really like coffee (orange juice).
I don't like omelettes very much.
The meal was very good.
I didn't like the steak (the green beans). It was too cold.

When you are eating …
Do you want a little cake (jam)?
No thank you, that's enough.
It was delicious, but I've had enough to drink (eat).
Some more tea (lemonade)?
Yes, with pleasure, I really like the cheese (the strawberries).
Pass me the bread (the salt), please.

To talk to the waiter (the waitress) …
[To attract the waiter's (waitress') attention.]
Have you chosen what to have?
I'll have the 120 franc menu.
To start with, the raw vegetable salad.
Then I'd like the chicken and chips.
For dessert, I'll have a pancake (peach).
We'll have a ham (pâté) sandwich.
And what would you like to drink?
Give us a bottle of mineral water, please.
Do you have some mustard (oil), please?

To ask for something …
What sorts of ice cream (yoghurts) have you got?
We have vanilla, chocolate and raspberry.
What exactly is the dish of the day?

After the meal …
The bill, please.
Excuse me, where is the telephone?
In the basement, next to the toilets.

Vous allez au restaurant avec des amis.

Write this conversation in full, then practise it with a partner.

Exam Practice

F **A**

1 Write these sentences correctly. Each answers a question a waiter/waitress might ask you.

  a J en'ai mep asbeau coupl esha rico tsverts.

  b Ler epa séta ittt rèsb on.

  c Jen' aipas aim éles har icotsv erts.

  d Ouia vecp lais irl ecaf ées ttr èsb on.

  e Jev oud rai sun epê che.

  f Jep rend slem enuàc entv ing tfra ncs.

  g Don nez-n ousu neb out eilled evi nrou ges'i lvou sp laît.

2 You need to ask lots of questions when you eat, and at least one in your role-play.
Write in French a question for each task below.

  a Ask if your friend likes orange juice.

  b Ask if your friend would like a little lemonade.

  c Ask if your friend would like some more jam.

  d Ask if your friend would like to drink.

  e Ask the waiter what sorts of cheeses he has.

  f Ask what the dish of the day is.

  g Ask the waiter if he has some mustard.

  h Ask where the toilets are.

F **B**

1 With the Teacher's Role covered, prepare this role-play in three minutes.

2 Practise with your partner until you are both perfect.

3 Write out the complete dialogue and underline any parts which you found difficult.
Concentrate on these when you learn it.

(Adapted from AQA/NEAB – 1998)

Teacher's Role	Candidate's Role
Tu es dans un restaurant, à Marseille. Moi, je suis le serveur (la serveuse). 1 Vous avez choisi? 2 Oui, et pour commencer? 3 Et ensuite? 4 Et comme boisson? 5 Oui, bien sûr.	You are in a restaurant in Marseille. 1 Say you will have the 130 franc menu. 2 You want tomato soup. 3 You want chicken and chips. 4 Ask the waiter if he has a bottle of mineral water. Your teacher will play the part of the waiter (waitress) and will speak first.

F/H **C**

1 Look at this flowchart. It shows how even a simple conversation can go in different directions. You need to listen to what the other person says and to be ready to respond to the unexpected.

2 See how many different conversations you can make up from the flowchart. Write at least four.

Vous commencez ici.

Tu aimes l'entrecôte?

Ah non, je n'aime pas la viande.

Oui, j'aime beaucoup l'entrecôte.

Quels légumes aimes-tu?

J'aime les frites et les haricots verts.

Je n'aime pas les petits pois. Mais j'aime les autres légumes.

Alors, prenons une entrecôte avec des frites et des haricots verts.

Alors, qu'est-ce que tu aimes?

J'aime bien le poisson et les légumes.

J'aime les œufs et le fromage.

Alors, prenons la soupe de tomates et les fruits de mer.

Alors, prenons une omelette au fromage avec des frites.

Pendant le repas …

Vous voulez un peu plus de chou-fleur (de carottes)?	Would you like a little more cauliflower (carrots)?
Oui, avec plaisir, c'est délicieux.	Yes, with pleasure, it's delicious.
Encore un peu de crème?	A little more cream?
Non merci, je n'aime pas beaucoup le jus de tomate (le chou).	No thanks, I don't like tomato juice (cabbage) very much.
Je voudrais encore un peu de sauce (de pommes de terre).	I'd like a little more gravy (potatoes).
Tu veux du sucre? Ça va comme ça, merci.	Would you like some sugar? That's enough, thank you.
Merci beaucoup pour ce repas délicieux.	Thank you very much for that delicious meal.
J'ai surtout aimé les fruits de mer.	I especially liked the seafood.
Tu as besoin d'un couteau (d'une fourchette, d'une cuillère)?	Do you need a knife (a fork, a spoon)?
Excusez-moi, mais je n'ai pas de tasse (de verre).	Excuse me, but I haven't got a cup (glass).

Pour réserver une table …

Je voudrais réserver une table.	I'd like to reserve a table.
Vous êtes combien? Je voudrais une table pour quatre personnes.	How many of you are there? I'd like a table for four.
Avez-vous une table pour trois personnes, en terrasse?	Have you got a table for three, on the terrace?
J'aimerais mieux être à l'intérieur. L'ambiance est si sympa.	I'd prefer to be inside. The atmosphere is so nice.
J'ai réservé une table non-fumeur pour huit heures.	I reserved a non-smoking table for 8 o'clock.
A quel nom? Au nom de White.	In what name? In the name of White.
Ça s'écrit comment?	How do you spell that?

(For help with the alphabet, see page 7.)

Quand il y a un problème …

Le service est compris?	Is service included?
Il n'y a pas une erreur?	Isn't there a mistake?
Je ne suis pas content(e). J'attends déjà depuis trente minutes.	I'm not pleased. I've already been waiting for 30 minutes.
J'ai commandé un café-crème, pas un chocolat chaud.	I ordered a white coffee, not a hot chocolate.
Il n'y avait pas assez d'oignons.	There weren't enough onions.
Je ne suis pas du tout satisfait(e). L'agneau (Le boeuf) était affreux.	I'm not at all satisfied. The lamb (beef) was terrible.
C'est très cher.	It's very expensive.

**Vous allez au restaurant avec un(e) ami(e) pour fêter votre anniversaire.
Est-ce que la soirée se passera bien?**

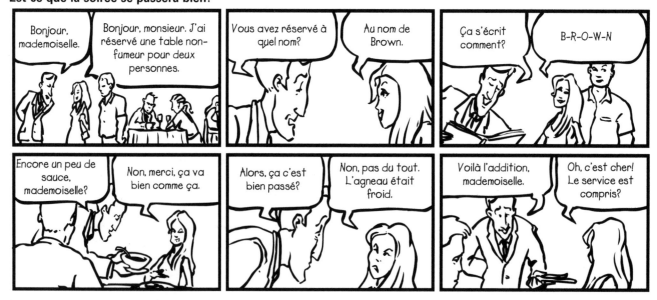

1 Practise the conversation with your partner until you know it really well.

2 Cover the cartoon and try to write the whole conversation using only these clues:

1  2 **BROWN** 3 B-R-O-W-N 4   5   6

Exam Practice

A

1 At Higher Tier, there is a short cue for each task, usually just one word. Read the cues below. Then read what the candidate says. Which sentences match which cues?

Cue	Candidate
1 Repas.	a J'aimerais mieux être à l'intérieur.
2 Table.	b Il n'y a pas une erreur?
3 Intérieur.	c L'ambiance était si sympa.
4 Problème.	d Le repas était vraiment délicieux.
5 Addition.	e Le bœuf était affreux.
6 Ambiance.	f Je voudrais réserver une table non-fumeur, pour trois personnes.

2 Now try to add something to each of the candidate's sentences, to give more information, e.g. *J'aimerais mieux être à l'intérieur, près de la fenêtre.*

B

1 Revise pages 22 and 24 and ask your partner to test you.

2 Cover the Teacher's Role and the Model Dialogue, and give yourself five minutes to prepare the role-play.

Remember:

- to decide whether you will use *tu* or *vous*.
- to think of questions the teacher might ask you for – ! – .

Candidate's Role

Your French friend is staying with you. You are both keen to go out for a meal, but you do not eat meat.
1 Votre opinion.
2 Votre suggestion.
3 Détails du restaurant.
4 !

Exam Tips

- In the second task, don't give the name of a restaurant, but describe the **sort** of restaurant you want to visit.
- Whenever you make a suggestion or express an opinion, you should also give a reason. You can either wait for the teacher to ask, or you can give the reason straight away. Remember always to plan a reason in your preparation time.
- The third task asks for details of the restaurant. Give at least two details but keep what you say simple.
- The unexpected question – ! – calls here for language from another topic. Examiners often combine two topics in one role-play, so be prepared for this and listen carefully to your teacher's questions.

Teacher's Role

1 On va en ville, prendre un steak?
(Candidate's task: to disagree about going for a steak and give a reason.)

2 Alors, où veux-tu aller manger?
(Candidate's task: to suggest another place to eat and say why he/she prefers to go there.)

3 Pourquoi pas? Il y a d'autres choses que tu aimes dans ce restaurant?
(Candidate's task: to say what else he/she likes about the place.)

4 D'accord, allons-y. Mais quand veux-tu y aller et comment?
(Candidate's task: to suggest when to go and how to get there.)

Model Dialogue

– On va en ville, prendre un steak?

– **Non, je ne peux pas manger de viande parce que je suis végétarien(ne).**

– Alors, où veux-tu aller manger?

– **Il y a un restaurant en ville où le poisson est très bon. Toi aussi, tu aimes bien le poisson, n'est-ce pas?**

– Pourquoi pas? Il y a d'autres choses que tu aimes dans ce restaurant?

– **Oui, l'ambiance est si sympa et ce n'est pas cher.**

– D'accord, allons-y. Mais quand veux-tu y aller et comment?

– **On peut réserver une table pour sept heures, si tu veux, et on peut y aller à pied parce que ce n'est pas loin.**

3 Study the Model Dialogue and notice how the candidate uses simple language and details. This is enough to score full marks.

4 Practise with a partner until you can both perform the candidate's part perfectly with the Model Dialogue covered.

Quand vous parlez de vous …

Comment t'appelles-tu?
Je m'appelle Michael.
Quel âge as-tu?
J'ai seize ans
Quelle est la date de ton anniversaire?
Mon anniversaire, c'est le vingt-sept juillet.
Qu'est-ce que tu aimes faire?
J'aime bien regarder la télé (écouter de la musique).
Je suis assez grand, j'ai les cheveux noirs et j'ai les yeux verts.
Je suis britannique.

When you are talking about yourself …

What's your name?
My name's Michael.
How old are you?
I'm 16.
What's the date of your birthday?
My birthday is on July 27th.
What do you like to do?
I really like watching TV (listening to music).
I'm quite tall, I have black hair and I have green eyes.
I'm British.

Quand vous parlez de votre famille …

Tu as des frères et des sœurs?
Je suis enfant unique.
J'ai un frère qui s'appelle Martin.
Tu peux le (la) décrire?
Il a quinze ans. Il est moins grand (plus grand) que moi.
Il a les cheveux longs et les yeux bleus. Il est gentil (bête).
Il est chauffeur (mécanicien).
J'ai une sœur qui s'appelle Kate.
Comment est-elle?
Elle a les cheveux courts. Elle aime faire du ski (monter à vélo).
Elle travaille dans une banque (un magasin).

When you are talking about your family …

Do you have any brothers or sisters?
I'm an only child.
I've got a brother whose name is Martin.
Can you describe him (her)?
He's 15. He's smaller (bigger) than me.
He has long hair and blue eyes. He's nice (stupid).
He's a driver (mechanic).
I have a sister called Kate.
What's she like?
She has short hair. She likes skiing (bike riding).
She works in a bank (shop).

Pour parler de vos animaux …

Tu as un animal, à la maison?
Oui, j'ai un chien (chat) qui s'appelle Roger.
Non, mais je voudrais bien avoir un cheval (un lapin).
Il est très gros (mince, drôle).

To talk about your pets …

Do you have a pet?
Yes, I've got a dog (cat) called Roger.
No, but I'd really like to have a horse (a rabbit).
He's very fat (thin, funny).

Quand vous rencontrez quelqu'un …

Bonjour, ça va?
Ça va bien, merci.
Enchanté(e).
Je te présente mon père (ma mère).
Entre (Entrez). Assieds-toi (Asseyez-vous).
Merci beaucoup pour votre hospitalité.
Vous avez été très gentils.

When you meet someone …

Hello, how are you?
I'm fine, thanks.
Pleased to meet you.
This is my father (mother).
Come in. Sit down.
Thank you very much for your hospitality.
You've all been very kind.

Votre correspondant français, Serge, vient passer huit jours chez vous.
Votre famille l'attend.

1 Work with a partner and practise reading these conversations aloud.
2 With your partner, make up and write down new conversations by changing the underlined words.

Exam Practice

 A

1 Cover the Dialogue and prepare the role-play.
2 Uncover the Dialogue and write it out in full.
3 Practise with a partner until you can both play both roles perfectly.

> *Exam Tip*
> Every answer you give can score two marks at Foundation Tier, as long as it communicates the message. So keep what you say short and simple: one piece of information in each answer will score full marks. Some candidates lose marks by trying to say too much and confusing the message.

Candidate's Role

You are on a beach in France and make friends with a young French person.
1 You want to know his/her name.
2 Ask how his/her name is spelt.
3 Say how old you are.
4 Say when your birthday is.

Your teacher will play the part of the French person and will speak first.

Dialogue
– B... .
– **C... t'... -t... ?**
– J... m'... Dominique.
– **Ç... s'... ... ?**
– D-O-M-I-N-I-Q-U-E.
– **J'... ... a... .**
– Et q... e... l... d... d... t... a... ?
– **M... a..., c'... l... ... .**
– Très bien.

(Adapted from AQA/NEAB – 1998)

 B

1 Cover the Model Dialogue and prepare your role.
2 Uncover the Model Dialogue and practise the role-play with your partner.

> *Exam Tip*
> Every answer can score three marks at Foundation/Higher Tier if you communicate all the information you are asked to give, without any big mistakes. Try to use a verb in every sentence. So, if your teacher asks: *Ton frère a quel âge?*, you should answer: *Il a quinze ans.*

Candidate's Role

You are at a camp site in France. You cannot find your sister. You are talking to the receptionist.
1 Give your sister's name and age.
2 Describe her eyes and hair.
3 Give two more details about what she looks like.
4 **!**

When you see this – **!** – you will have to respond to something which you have not prepared. Your teacher will play the part of the receptionist and will speak first.

Model Dialogue
– Comment s'appelle votre sœur et quel âge a-t-elle?
– **Elle s'appelle Mary et elle a onze ans.**
– Vous pouvez la décrire?
– **Oui, elle a les yeux verts et les cheveux noirs.**
– Vous pouvez me donner deux autres détails?
– **Elle est moins grande que moi et elle est très mince.**
– Quand avez-vous vu votre sœur la dernière fois?
– **Ce matin, vers dix heures.**
– Nous allons bientôt la trouver.

(Adapted from AQA/NEAB – 1998)

 C

1 Revise page 26 and the Exam Tips on pages 9, 13, 15 and 19.
2 Cover the Teacher's Role and prepare your role in five minutes.
3 Practise the role-play with your partner, then take turns to ask the teacher's questions again and to answer them about you and your families. Write these new conversations.

Teacher's Role

Tu es en France. Moi, je suis ton ami(e).
1 Tu as une grande famille?
2 Tu peux me décrire ta sœur?
3 Ta sœur, que fait-elle dans la vie?
4 Et qu'est-ce qu'elle aime faire, ta sœur?
5 Moi, j'aime faire du ski.

Candidate's Role

You have met a French boy/girl at the disco.
1 Tell him/her that you have a sister and two brothers.
2 Describe your sister's hair and eyes.
3 Tell him/her what your sister does for a living.
4 **!**

Your teacher will play the part of the French boy/girl and will speak first.

(Adapted from AQA/NEAB – 1998)

Quand vous parlez de votre famille …	When you are talking about your family …
Ton frère est marié?	Is your brother married?
Ma sœur est célibataire.	My sister is single.
Mes parents sont divorcés depuis quatre ans.	My parents have been divorced for four years.
Mon frère aîné a deux enfants, une fille de cinq ans et un fils de neuf mois.	My older brother has two children, a daughter of 5 and a son of 9 months.

Pour dire où vous habitez …	To say where you live …
Mes cousins habitent au 36 Edward Street.	My cousins live at 36 Edward Street.
Comment s'écrit le nom de la rue?	How do you spell the street name?
Voici mon adresse: le quarante-huit, rue de la Gare.	Here is my address: 48 Station Street.

Pour décrire votre famille …	To describe your family …
Comment trouves-tu ta grand-mère (ton grand-père)?	How do you find your grandmother (grandfather)?
Elle est toujours douce et optimiste.	She's always gentle and optimistic.
Je la trouve très bien. Elle s'intéresse à tout.	I find her very fine. She takes an interest in everything.
Ma sœur aînée est parfois paresseuse et désagréable.	My older sister is sometimes lazy and disagreeable.
Tu t'entends bien avec ton beau-père (ta belle-mère)?	Do you get on well with your stepfather (stepmother)?
Je m'entends bien (mal) avec mes parents.	I get on well (badly) with my parents.

Pour parler de vos problèmes …	To talk about your problems …
Je me dispute souvent avec mes amis.	I often quarrel with my friends.
Mes parents ne me comprennent pas. Mon père est trop sévère.	My parents don't understand me. My dad is too strict.
Qu'est-ce que je peux faire?	What can I do?
Mes professeurs me critiquent tout le temps.	My teachers are always criticising me.
Je veux m'amuser mais ma mère ne me laisse jamais sortir.	I want to enjoy myself but my mum never lets me go out.
Je dois toujours être de retour à la maison avant vingt-deux heures.	I always have to be home before 10 p.m.
Puis-je appeler le médecin?	May I call the doctor?
Excuse-moi, c'était de ma faute.	Sorry, it was my fault.
Je m'excuse. J'ai oublié de t'écrire.	I'm sorry. I've forgotten to write to you.

Vous êtes chez votre amie, en France. Votre amie veut trouver une correspondante pour sa cousine qui voudrait faire un échange avec une jeune britannique.

(Adapted from AQA/NEAB – 1998)

1 Practise reading this conversation aloud with your partner.
2 Partner A plays the French girl's part. Partner B covers the cartoon and uses the instructions on the right to play the other part:

You are staying with your French friend. Your friend wants to find a partner for his/her cousin who wants to go on an exchange visit to Britain.

- Votre suggestion.
- Les activités.
- Moment de l'année.
- !

Exam Practice

A

1 Revise the Exam Tips on pages 11, 17, 21 and 25.
2 Cover the Teacher's Role and prepare this role-play.
3 Look at the Teacher's Role and work with a partner until you can both play both parts perfectly – giving all the details, with no mistakes or ambiguity.

Candidate's Role

You are looking for a penfriend for your younger brother, Matthew. Your French friend has collected some details for you. You are looking together at the information on the right.
1 Frère
2 Jean – pourquoi pas.
3 Pierre – pourquoi.
4 !
Your teacher will play the part of your friend and will speak first.

(Adapted from AQA/NEAB – 1998)

My brother, Matthew: 14 years old, likes sport, computers, pop music.

PIERRE
15 ANS
FOOTBALL
SKI
MUSIQUE POP

JEAN
14 ANS
LA MUSIQUE CLASSIQUE
VÉLO
TÉLÉVISION

Teacher's Role

1 Il est comment, ton frère Matthew?
   (Candidate's task: to give at least three details about Matthew.)
2 A mon avis, il s'entendrait bien avec Jean, n'est-ce pas?
   (Candidate's task: to reject Jean, giving a reason.)
3 Alors, que penses-tu de Pierre?
   (Candidate's task: to explain why Pierre is a good penfriend for Matthew.)
4 A ton avis, pourquoi est-ce une bonne idée d'avoir un correspondant?
   (Candidate's task: to explain why it is a good idea to have a penfriend.)

B

1 Now read the conversation on the right, based on the role-play in A. Mark each answer out of four and take off one mark:
   - for every mistake;
   - each time the candidate omits a detail which is asked for;
   - any time the candidate is ambiguous.
2 This candidate lost one mark for the answer to no. 1, one mark for the answer to no. 2 and one mark for the answer to no. 3. Can you explain why?
3 Write the first three answers so that they would all score four marks.

1 Il est comment, ton frère Matthew?

– **Il a quatorze ans, il aime le sport et il s'intéresse aux ordinateurs.**

2 A mon avis, il s'entendrait bien avec Jean, n'est-ce pas?

– **Non, je ne pense pas. Matthew aime la musique pop.**

3 Alors, que penses-tu de Pierre?

– **Je pense que Pierre serait un bon correspondant pour Matthew. Pierre aime le sport et le musique pop, comme Matthew.**

4 A ton avis, pourquoi est-ce une bonne idée d'avoir un correspondant?

– **Parce que j'aime beaucoup lire tes lettres.**

Quand vous parlez de vos passe-temps …
Quel est ton passe-temps préféré?
J'aime beaucoup jouer de la guitare (du piano).
Tu aimes le sport?
Mon sport préféré, c'est le cyclisme (la pêche).
Je suis membre d'un club d'équitation (de natation).
Je fais de la gymnastique une fois par semaine.
Le week-end dernier, j'ai joué au basket.
Moi aussi, j'aime danser.
Moi, je préfère faire des promenades.

When you talk about your pastimes …
What is your favourite pastime?
I like playing the guitar (piano) a lot.
Do you like sport?
My favourite sport is cycling (fishing).
I'm a member of a riding (swimming) club.
I do gymnastics once a week.
Last weekend, I played basketball.
I also like dancing.
I prefer to go walking.

Pour dire ce que vous avez fait …
Qu'est-ce que tu as fait le week-end dernier?
Samedi matin, j'ai fait les magasins.
L'après-midi, j'ai été au bord de la mer.
Dimanche, j'ai joué au cricket (au tennis).
A mon avis, c'était un bon match.
Pourquoi?
Nous avons bien joué et nous avons gagné.

To say what you have done …
What did you do last weekend?
On Saturday morning, I went to the shops.
In the afternoon, I went to the seaside.
On Sunday, I played cricket (tennis).
In my opinion, it was a good match.
Why?
We played well and we won.

Quand vous sortez …
Le stade (Le centre de loisirs) ouvre à quelle heure?
Le théâtre ouvre (ferme) à dix-neuf heures.
Le concert (La séance) commence (finit) à quinze heures.
La pièce (Le film) dure deux heures.
Ça coûte combien? Quarante francs.
Une personne, s'il vous plaît.
Vous êtes combien? Un adulte et deux enfants.
Il y a une réduction pour les étudiants.

When you go out …
At what time does the stadium (leisure centre) open?
The theatre opens (closes) at 7 p.m.
The concert (performance) starts (finishes) at 3 p.m.
The play (film) lasts 2 hours.
How much does it cost? 40 francs.
(A ticket for) one person, please.
How many of you are there? One adult and two children.
There is a reduction for students.

Pour parler de votre argent de poche …
Tes parents te donnent combien d'argent de poche?
Mes parents me donnent cinq livres par semaine.
Comment le dépenses-tu? J'achète des CD (des vêtements).
Je travaille dans un magasin (une usine) pour gagner de l'argent.
Je gagne trente livres par jour.

To talk about your pocket money …
How much pocket money do your parents give you?
My parents give me £5 per week.
How do you spend it? I buy CDs (clothes).
I work in a shop (a factory) to earn some money.
I earn £30 a day.

Vous êtes en France et vous allez au centre de loisirs avec des amis.

(Adapted from AQA/NEAB – 1998)

1 Read the conversation and practise it with your partner.
2 Student A covers the cartoon and plays the girl's part, using the instructions below.
 Student B plays the part of the man in the leisure centre and reads his lines.
 You are at a leisure centre in France.

- Say you would like to play tennis.
- Say there are two adults and one child.
- Say that you want to play at 4 o'clock.
- Ask how much it costs.

Exam Practice

F A

1 Cover the French sentences on the right below.
2 Prepare the two role-plays in six minutes.
3 Write the sentences in the correct order to make up the two role-plays.
4 Practise them with your partner, until you can do them perfectly.

Candidate's Roles

A

You are talking to your French friend about work.
1 Say that you work in a factory.
2 You earn £30 a day.
3 Say you buy cassettes with your money.
4 Ask if your friend likes music.

B

Your French friend is staying at your house.
1 Ask if your friend likes sport.
2 Say that you would like to go to a rugby match.
3 Say it starts at 2 o'clock.
4 Say it costs £9.

(Adapted from AQA/NEAB – 1998)

Exam Tip

Always read the role-play instructions very carefully and make sure that you say what you are told to say. For example:

• when the instructions say: Say that you like …, you must say *J'aime …*

• when the instructions say: Say that you would like to …, you must say *Je voudrais …*

– Salut!
– Tu aimes le sport?
– Ça commence à quatorze heures.
– Ce n'est pas trop cher.
– Bonne idée. A quelle heure?
– C'est combien?
– Je voudrais aller à un match de rugby.
– Neuf livres.
– Oui, j'aime beaucoup le sport.
– Où travailles-tu, le samedi?
– Trente livres par jour.
– Tu as de la chance, toi.
– Tu aimes la musique?
– J'achète des cassettes.
– Tu gagnes combien?
– Je travaille dans une usine.
– Qu'est-ce que tu fais de ton argent?
– Oui, j'adore la musique.

F/H B

1 Cover the Teacher's Role and Model Dialogue, and prepare the role-play.
2 Look at the Teacher's Role and practise the role-play with a partner.
3 Look at the Model Dialogue and compare it with what you said. Then practise it until you are both perfect.

Exam Tips

• Think what the teacher will ask you for the **!** .

• When you answer this task, be sure to give two details.

Teacher's Role

Tu es au théâtre, en France.
Moi, je suis le caissier (la caissière).
1 Bonjour. Vous êtes combien?
2 D'accord.
3 Oui, il y a une réduction de trente pour cent. Vous voulez voir quelle séance?
4 La pièce dure deux heures.

> **THEATRE MUNICIPAL**
> *L'Alouette*
> de **Jean Anouilh**
> Séances 14h15 et 20h30
> Tous les jours.

Candidate's Role

You are at a French theatre, buying tickets.
1 Say that there is one adult and two students.
2 Ask if there is a reduction for students.
3 **!**
4 Ask how long the play lasts.

Your teacher will play the part of the cashier and will speak first.

(Adapted from AQA/NEAB – 1998)

Model Dialogue

– Bonjour. Vous êtes combien?

– Il y a un adulte et deux enfants.

– D'accord.

– Il y a une réduction pour les étudiants?

– Oui, il y a une réduction de 30%. Vous voulez quelle séance?

– La séance de vingt heures trente, demain. La pièce dure combien de temps?

– La pièce dure deux heures.

Pour exprimer vos opinions …

Je préfère faire de la voile (jouer aux échecs).
Je n'aime pas du tout faire de l'équitation.
Quel est ton groupe (acteur) préféré?
Le concert (jeu) était très bon (affreux).
Je me suis ennuyé(e) parce que la pièce était trop lente.
J'aimerais mieux faire une randonnée.

To express your opinions …

I prefer sailing (playing chess).
I don't like horse riding at all.
Which is your favourite group (actor)?
The concert (game) was very good (awful).
I was bored because the play was too slow.
I'd prefer to go for a walk.

Pour parler des clubs …

Tu es membre d'un club?
Le jeudi soir, je vais à un club de jeunes. On joue au billard anglais.
Je suis membre d'un club (d'une équipe) de rugby (hockey).

To talk about clubs …

Are you a member of a club?
On Thursday evenings, I go to a youth club. We play snooker.
I'm a member of a rugby (hockey) club (team).

Pour parler des excursions …

Avez-vous des renseignements (dépliants) sur les excursions dans la région?
Vous pourriez aller voir la côte. Quand voulez-vous partir?
Mercredi prochain. Le prix des visites (des repas) est compris?
On pourrait aller au musée.

To talk about excursions …

Do you have any information (leaflets) about excursions in the region?
You could go and see the coast. When do you want to go?
Next Wednesday. Is the price of visits (meals) included?
We could go to the museum.

Pour parler de l'argent …

Tu as combien d'argent de poche?
Je n'ai que quatre livres par semaine.
Tu trouves que c'est assez? Non, je n'ai jamais assez d'argent.
Je sors trop souvent et j'achète trop de magazines.
Oui, j'ai assez d'argent.
Je sors peu et mes parents achètent tous mes vêtements.
Je fais des économies.
Pour aller en vacances avec mes amis l'année prochaine.
Je ne vais en discothèque que quand j'ai un billet gratuit.

To talk about money …

How much pocket money do you have?
I only have £4 per week.
Do you find that's enough? No, I never have enough money.
I go out too often and I buy too many magazines.
Yes, I have enough money.
I don't go out much and my parents buy all my clothes.
I'm saving some money.
To go on holiday with my friends next year.
I only go to the disco when I have a free ticket.

Vous avez des billets gratuits pour une nouvelle discothèque. Vous invitez votre ami français à y aller avec vous.

(Adapted from AQA/NEAB – 1998)

1 Practise this conversation with a partner and learn both parts.
2 Partner A acts the girl's part using only the cues below.
   Partner B reads the boy's lines from the cartoon.

   • Où aller.   • Prix.   • Description.   • !

RITZ DISCO
Competitions
Restaurant facilities
Large video screen

Exam Practice

A

> ***Exam Tips***
> - The flowchart shows how a set of instructions can produce two different conversation, so it is important to listen carefully to what your teacher says.
> - Exam role-plays try to be like real life, and you should be able to anticipate what people may say in a given situation. Use your knowledge of real life to guess what you may be asked when you see the ! and to work out how you will reply.

1 Read these instructions and prepare your part.

You are staying with your friend in Belgium. You want to go out this weekend. Your friend suggests going to a football match but you are not keen.

- La suggestion de votre ami(e).
- Votre suggestion.
- Détails de votre suggestion.
- **!**

Your teacher will play the part of your friend and will speak first.

(Adapted from AQA/NEAB – 1998)

2 Follow the flowchart and write two different conversations based on it.

3 Act out your two role-plays with a partner.

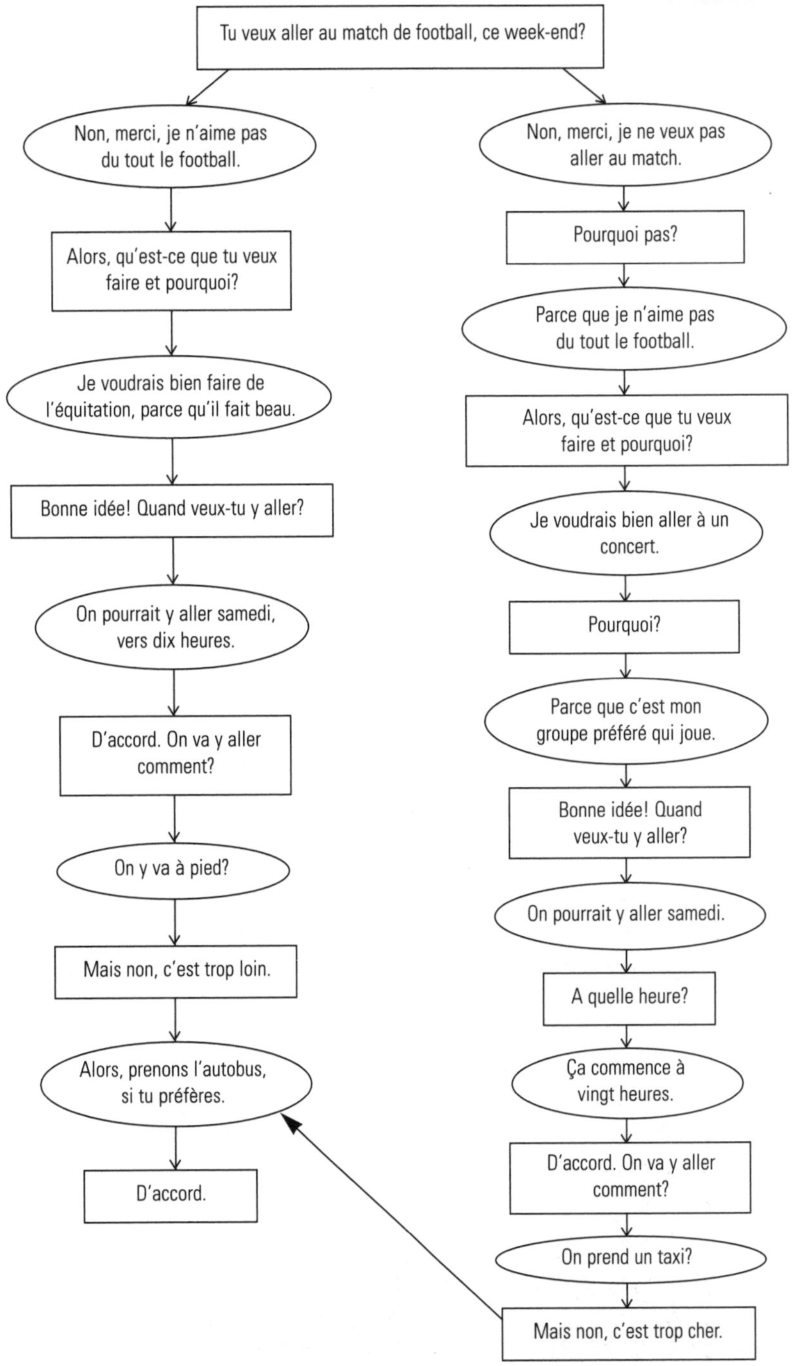
Tu veux aller au match de football, ce week-end?
Non, merci, je n'aime pas du tout le football.
Alors, qu'est-ce que tu veux faire et pourquoi?
Je voudrais bien faire de l'équitation, parce qu'il fait beau.
Bonne idée! Quand veux-tu y aller?
On pourrait y aller samedi, vers dix heures.
D'accord. On va y aller comment?
On y va à pied?
Mais non, c'est trop loin.
Alors, prenons l'autobus, si tu préfères.
D'accord.
Non, merci, je ne veux pas aller au match.
Pourquoi pas?
Parce que je n'aime pas du tout le football.
Alors, qu'est-ce que tu veux faire et pourquoi?
Je voudrais bien aller à un concert.
Pourquoi?
Parce que c'est mon groupe préféré qui joue.
Bonne idée! Quand veux-tu y aller?
On pourrait y aller samedi.
A quelle heure?
Ça commence à vingt heures.
D'accord. On va y aller comment?
On prend un taxi?
Mais non, c'est trop cher.

B

1 Revise everything on pages 12, 14, 30 and 32. Ask your partner to test you.

2 Cover the Teacher's Role and prepare your role.

3 Uncover the Teacher's Role and practise the conversation with a partner.

4 Write the conversation in full.

> ***Exam Tip***
> Many role-plays require you to use French from more than one topic. You need to be ready for this.

Teacher's Role

1 Qu'est-ce qu'on va faire, ce soir? *(Candidate's task: to explain that you are going to a friend's house.)*
2 Il/Elle est comment, ton ami(e)? *(Candidate's task: to explain what his/her friend is like.)*
3 Et qu'est-ce qu'on va faire, chez ton ami(e)? *(Candidate's task: to explain what you are going to do at the friend's house.)*
4 On rentrera à quelle heure et comment? *(Candidate's task: to explain at what time and how you will return home.)*

Candidate's Role

Your French friend is staying with you. You are going to a friend's house this evening but your French friend is not keen to go.

1 Votre suggestion.
2 Détails de ton ami(e) britannique.
3 Activités.
4 **!**

Your teacher will play the part of your friend and will speak first.

(Adapted from AQA/NEAB – 1998)

Pour inviter ...
On va faire une promenade? Quelle bonne idée!
Je vais au cinéma, tu veux venir avec moi?
Je t'invite à ma boum, samedi prochain.
On va au match. Tu veux y aller?
Je regrette, mais je dois rester à la maison.

To invite ...
Shall we go for a walk? What a good idea!
I'm going to the cinema, do you want to come with me?
I'm inviting you to my party, next Saturday.
We're going to the match. Do you want to go?
I'm sorry, but I have to stay at home.

Pour prendre rendez-vous ...
On se voit où?
Si on se voyait devant la discothèque?
On se voit à quelle heure?
On se voit à vingt heures?
Avec plaisir.
Je m'excuse, mais je ne peux pas.

To arrange to meet ...
Where shall we meet?
How about meeting in front of the disco?
At what time shall we meet?
Shall we meet at 8 p.m.?
With pleasure.
I'm sorry, but I can't.

Quand vous allez au cinéma ...
Qu'est-ce qu'on passe au cinéma, ce soir?
C'est quelle sorte de film?
C'est un film d'épouvante (un film comique).
Génial! La dernière séance commence à quelle heure?
C'est combien, s'il vous plaît?
Trois places pour la salle quatre.
Le film finit à quelle heure? Vers minuit.

When you go to the cinema ...
What's on at the cinema, this evening?
What sort of film is it?
It's a horror (comedy) film.
Great! At what time does the last performance start?
How much is it, please?
Three for screen 4.
At what time does the film finish? At about midnight.

Pour parler du spectacle ...
C'était vraiment chouette!
Tu as aimé le film (concert)?
C'était bien (intéressant).
Je suis d'accord avec toi.

To talk about the show ...
It was really great!
Did you like the film (concert)?
It was good (interesting).
I agree with you.

Quand vous restez à la maison ...
Qu'est-ce qu'on fait, ce soir?
Qu'est-ce qu'il y a à la télé?
Il y a une émission de musique classique (les informations).
Qu'est-ce qu'on peut faire à part ça? Tu aimes les jeux-vidéo?

When you stay at home ...
What shall we do, this evening?
What's on TV?
It's a classical music programme (the news).
What else can we do? Do you like video games?

Vous voulez aller au cinéma avec une amie française.

(Adapted from AQA/NEAB – 1998)

1 Practise the conversation with a partner and learn the boy's part.
2 Cover the cartoon and write the conversation below.
3 Check with the cartoon that you have written it correctly.

Jeune fille: Qu'est-ce qu'on fait, ce soir?
Garçon: (Suggest going to the cinema.)
Jeune fille: D'accord. Qu'est-ce qu'on passe au cinéma?
Garçon: (Say that there is a comedy.)
Jeune fille: D'accord, on se voit où et quand?

Garçon: (Say when and where you will meet.)
Jeune fille: D'accord, si tu veux.
Garçon: (Tell her you are going to the café afterwards.)
Jeune fille: Quelle bonne idée!

Exam Practice

 A

1 Read the Candidate's and Teacher's Roles.
2 The phrases you need to complete the candidate's
tasks are on the right, but they are in the wrong order.
Write out the role-play in full, then practise it with a
partner.

Il faut prendre l'autobus numéro dix.

Il y a un bon film.

Le film commence à vingt heures trente.

Tu veux aller au cinéma?

Teacher's Role

Tu parles avec ton ami(e) québécois(e). Moi, je suis ton
ami(e).
1 Alors, qu'est-ce qu'on fait, ce soir?
2 Quelle bonne idée! Qu'est-ce qu'on passe?
3 D'accord. Le film commence à quelle heure?
4 Comment va-t-on y aller?
5 D'accord.

Candidate's Role

Your friend from Quebec is staying with you and you are
arranging to go out.
1 Ask if your friend wants to go to the cinema.
2 There's a good film on.
3 The film starts at 8.30.
4 You need to catch a number 10 bus.

(Adapted from AQA/NEAB – 1997)

 B

Prepare this role-play in four minutes, then complete the
candidate's answers on the right, making sure you give
all the information required. Write all the answers in full.

Exam Tip
Remember to read the instructions carefully and to listen
carefully to your teacher's questions. Then give all the
information you are asked to give.

Candidate's Role

On holiday in France, you see an
advertisement for a jazz concert.

> **Palais des Congrès**
> Concert de Jazz
> 20h30 – 22h15

1 You telephone a French friend to suggest you go and see it.
2 Your friend wants to know what time the concert starts and ends.
3 !
4 Find out if your friend prefers to go on Friday or Saturday.

(AQA/NEAB – 1998)

– Allô, oui.
– **Il y a un concert de jazz, ce soir …**
– Le concert commence et finit à quelle heure?
– **Il commence à vingt heures trente …**
– Et ça coûte combien?
– **Ça coûte cinquante …**
– Ce n'est pas trop cher.
– **Tu préfères y aller vendredi …**
– Je préfère y aller vendredi.

 **C**

1 Revise the phrases on page 34 and ask your partner to test you.
2 Cover the Model Dialogue and prepare your role in four minutes.
3 Practise the role-play with a partner until you can both play the Candidate's Role
perfectly. Partner A then covers the Model Dialogue and plays the candidate.
Partner B uses the Model Dialogue to play the teacher.

Candidate's Role

Your Belgian friend is staying with you and wants to
watch television.
1 Ask your friend what type of programme he/she likes.
2 Say that there is an interesting documentary on at
8 o'clock.
3 Ask if he/she prefers to go to the cinema.
4 !
Your teacher will play the part of your friend and will
speak first.

Model Dialogue
– J'aimerais bien regarder la télé, ce soir.
– **Tu aimes quelle sort d'émission?**
– J'aime bien les émissions sur les animaux.
– **Il y a un documentaire intéressant à vingt heures.**
– Ça ne m'intéresse pas beaucoup.
– **Tu préfères aller au cinéma?**
– Quelle bonne idée! Et qu'est-ce qu'on fait avant d'aller au
cinéma?
– **On pourrait faire une promenade ou écouter les informations.**
– D'accord.

Pour parler de ce qu'on peut faire ...

On peut jouer au golf (aux cartes) ici?
J'aimerais bien aller danser: c'est possible?
On pourrait visiter le musée, si tu préfères.
Qu'est-ce qu'on peut faire, demain soir?
Il y a une bonne pièce, au théâtre.
Tu pourrais aller faire les magasins, à Londres.
On se voit à midi?
Malheureusement, je ne suis pas libre.
Si on se rencontrait cet après-midi?

To talk about what you can do ...

Can you play golf (cards) here?
I'd really like to go dancing: is it possible?
We could visit the museum, if you prefer.
What can we do, tomorrow evening?
There's a good play on, at the theatre.
You could go shopping in London.
Shall we meet at midday?
Unfortunately, I'm not free.
How about meeting this afternoon?

Pour dire ce que vous en pensez ...

Comment avez-vous trouvé la pièce?
C'était extraordinaire (formidable).
J'ai vu un bon film, la semaine dernière.
C'était en version française ou en version originale?
C'était sous-titré.
De quoi s'agit-il?
Il s'agit du désastre du Titanic.
Le héros est un jeune homme pauvre qui tombe amoureux d'une fille très riche.
A la fin, l'héroïne est sauvée mais le garçon meurt.
C'est très triste (romantique). C'est mon film préféré.
Je préfère les films d'amour (les films policiers).
C'était passionnant (drôle).

To say what you think about it ...

How did you find the play?
It was extraordinary (great).
I saw a good film last week.
Was it in the French version or the original version?
It was sub-titled.
What's it about?
It's about the Titanic disaster.
The hero is a poor young man who falls in love with a very rich girl.
At the end, the heroine is saved but the boy dies.
It's very sad (romantic). It's my favourite film.
I prefer love films (detective films).
It was exciting (funny).

Vous avez accepté une invitation pour aller voir votre ami, à Paris. Mais, malheureusement, vous ne pouvez plus y aller. Vous téléphonez à votre ami pour lui expliquer la situation.

(Adapted from AQA/NEAB – 1998)

1 Read the cartoon and the role-play instructions below.
2 Use the gapped sentences in the box to write the girl's part.
3 Practise the conversation with a partner.

You had planned to visit a friend in Paris but now you can't go. You phone him to explain the situation.

1 Vos nouvelles.   3 Votre suggestion.
2 Pourquoi.   4 !

1 N..., mal... j... n... p... plus v... à P... .
2 Ma mère e... mal... et j... dois m'occuper d'e... .
3 T... p... a... à L... et t... p... f... l... m... .
4 A m... av..., l... m... m... , c'... Noël.
5 P... qu... tout le monde e... heureux.
6 D'... , à b... .

Exam Practice

A

1 Revise carefully all the phrases on pages 34 and 36: make sure that you know them all really well.

2 To learn key phrases and to practise role-plays, you could make a 'word sun' of answers to key questions.

3 Photograph the 'word sun' on the right in your mind, cover it and then try to make a perfect copy. Compare your copy with the original and continue until they are both identical.

4 Make up your own 'word sun'. Write a relevant phrase at the end of each line. Then cover it and make a perfect copy.

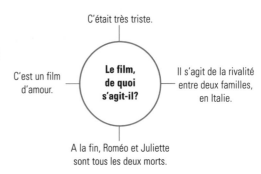

Exam Tip
Make sure that you can talk about the main features of a film or play you have seen. Learn four or five sentences to describe it and to express and justify an opinion about it.

B

1 Cover the Teacher's Role and the Answers. Prepare the role-play in five minutes. Remember to give all the details you are asked for.

2 Look at the Teacher's Role and check that you have prepared all the tasks fully. Write out your completed role-play.

Candidate's Role

You are talking to a French friend about what to do at the weekend.
You look in the newspaper and see the following details about what's on.

Stade Municipal
Match de football entre
le Racing de Paris et Montpellier,
dimanche à 15 heures.
Entrée 80 francs

Théâtre Molière
L'année dernière, une pièce comique de Michel Dutout
Tous les jours, à 19 heures 30.
Entrée 40 francs.

Cinéma Vog
Le retour de *Quatre mariages et un enterrement*
Séances à 14 heures, 17 heures et 20 heures.
Entrée 45 francs (réduction pour étudiants).

Spectacles
Opéra Debussy
Concert de Berlioz et Ravel.
Jeudi à samedi, à 20 heures.
Entrée 50 francs (adultes) et 30 francs (moins de 15 ans).

You are not keen on sport. You need to reach an agreement with your friend about what to do.
Your teacher will play the part of your friend and will speak first.

(Adapted from AQA/NEAB – 1998)

Teacher's Role

1 Tu veux aller au match de football, ce week-end?
(Candidate's task: to disagree about going to a football match and to give a reason.)

2 Alors, où veux-tu aller?
(Candidate's task: to suggest an alternative place to go, and say why.)

3 D'accord. On se voit où et à quelle heure?
(Candidate's task: to suggest a time and place to meet.)

4 Et qu'est-ce qu'on peut faire après?
(Candidate's task: to suggest something to do afterwards.)

Answers

1 Non, merci, je ne veux pas aller au match de football.
(Candidate should also give a reason.)

2 Si on allait au cinéma Vog?
(Candidate should also give a reason.)

3 On se voit devant le cinéma?
(Candidate should also suggest a time to meet.)

4 On pourrait aller au café, si tu veux.

3 Read the Answers and compare them with yours. The candidate here has not always given enough details. Add more to answers 1–3 to score full marks.

Pour décrire votre ville …

Où habites-tu? J'habite à Manchester.

C'est une grande (petite) ville dans le nord (sud, est, ouest) de l'Angleterre (du Pays de Galles).

Tu peux me décrire la ville?

La ville n'est pas belle mais elle est intéressante.

Qu'est-ce qu'il y a à voir?

Il y a un vieux château.

C'est une ville industrielle (moderne, tranquille).

La région est jolie.

To describe your town …

Where do you live? I live in Manchester.

It is a big (small) town in the north (south, east, west) of England (of Wales).

Can you describe the town?

The town isn't beautiful but it is interesting.

What is there to see?

There's an old castle.

It's an industrial (modern, quiet) town.

The region is pretty.

Quand vous montrez votre ville à des visiteurs …

Que penses-tu de la ville?

J'aime bien habiter ici.

Il y a beaucoup de choses à faire pour les jeunes.

Je n'aime pas la ville. Il n'y a rien à faire.

C'est ennuyeux (moche).

When you show your town to visitors …

What do you think of the town?

I really like living here.

There's a lot for young people to do.

I don't like the town. There's nothing to do.

It's boring (ugly).

Pour aller en ville …

Comment peut-on aller en ville?

On peut prendre l'autobus (le métro) pour aller dans le centre-ville.

Il y a un train tous les combien?

Toutes les vingt minutes.

Ça prend combien de temps?

Un quart d'heure.

To get into town …

How can you get into town?

You can take the bus (the underground) to get to the town centre.

How often is there a train?

Every 20 minutes.

How long does it take?

A quarter of an hour.

Pour parler des fêtes …

Que fais-tu, à Noël?

Nous ne fêtons pas Noël.

J'envoie des cartes à mes amis.

Pour mon anniversaire, j'ai des cadeaux.

Pour mon dernier anniversaire, j'ai fait une grande boum.

To talk about holidays and festivals …

What do you do at Christmas?

We don't celebrate Christmas.

I send cards to my friends.

For my birthday, I have presents.

For my last birthday, I had a big party.

Pour parler du temps …

Quel temps fait-il, en hiver (en été)?

Il fait assez froid, en hiver. Il fait beau, en été.

Il pleut souvent, au printemps (en automne).

Il fait souvent mauvais temps.

A Pâques, il fait chaud.

To talk about the weather …

What's the weather like in winter (in summer)?

It's quite cold in winter. It's nice in summer.

It often rains in spring (autumn).

The weather is often bad.

At Easter, it's hot.

Vous êtes chez votre ami, en France, et vous parlez de votre ville.

1 Practise this conversation with a partner and learn the English boy's part.

2 Take turns to ask the questions and to give your own answers about where you live.

Exam Practice

F **A**

1 Use this table to make up as many different answers as you can to the question:
Où habites-tu?

J'habite à ... C'est ...	une grande ville	dans le nord	de l'Angleterre.
	une petite ville	dans le sud	du Pays de Galles.
	une ville industrielle	dans l'ouest	de l'Irlande du Nord.
	une ville moderne	dans l'est	de l'Ecosse.
	un vieux village	dans le centre	

2 Use this table to make up as many answers as you can to the question:
Qu'est-ce qu'il y a à voir?

Il y a	un vieux	château.
	une belle	cathédrale.
	de belles	montagnes.
	de grands	église.
		musée.
		magasins.

3 And now make up as many answers as you can to this final question: *Quel temps fait-il?*

Il fait	froid	au printemps.
	chaud	en été.
	beau	en automne.
	mauvais	en hiver.

4 Finally, write three conversations, using the questions and different answers to them.

F **B**

1 Prepare this role-play and practise it with a partner.
2 Write out the whole conversation and learn it.

Teacher's Role	**Candidate's Role**
Tu parles de là où tu habites avec ton ami(e) français(e). Moi, je suis ton ami(e).	You are talking with your French friend about where you live.
1 Où habites-tu?	1 Say you live in the south of England.
2 Tu peux me décrire la ville?	2 Say it is an industrial town.
3 On peut visiter les musées et on peut aller au cinéma.	3 Ask what there is to do in your friend's town.
4 Quel temps fait-il, en hiver?	4 Say it's quite cold.

F/H **C**

1 Cover the Teacher's Role below. Work with your partner to decide on the two most likely questions your teacher might ask at the end. Then prepare good answers.
2 Uncover the Teacher's Role. Did you guess the question?
3 Practise the role-play with your partner until you are both word perfect.
4 Write out the whole conversation and learn it.

Teacher's Role	**Candidate's Role**
Tu es chez ton ami(e), en Suisse. Moi, je suis ton ami(e).	You are talking with a Swiss friend about birthdays.
1 Quelle est la date de ton anniversaire?	1 Tell him/her when your birthday is.
2 Qu'est-ce qui se passe le jour de ton anniversaire?	2 Tell him/her that you get presents and cards.
3 Que fais-tu pour fêter ton anniversaire?	3 Say that you have a big party.
4 Qu'est-ce que tu as fait pour ton dernier anniversaire?	4 !
	Your teacher will play the part of your friend and will speak first.

Pour faire des comparaisons ...

Leeds est plus grand que Bordeaux.
Il fait moins froid, en hiver.
A Gignac, l'industrie (l'agriculture) est plus importante.
Il y a plus d'habitants ici qu'à Boulogne.
Ici, c'est plus bruyant (tranquille).

To make comparisons ...

Leeds is bigger than Bordeaux.
It's not as cold, in winter.
In Gignac, industry (agriculture) is more important.
There are more inhabitants here than in Boulogne.
It's noisier (quieter) here.

Pour exprimer vos opinions ...

J'aime vivre ici parce que le paysage est très joli.
Je n'aime pas vivre ici parce que c'est vraiment moche.
Il y a beaucoup d'industrie.
Ici, en hiver, le climat est humide et froid.
Là, le climat est sec et chaud.
J'aimerais mieux vivre en France (en Belgique, en Suisse).
Il y a des montagnes et des lacs.

To express your opinions ...

I like living here because the countryside is very pretty.
I don't like living here because it's really ugly.
There is a lot of industry.
Here, in winter, the climate is damp and cold.
There the climate is dry and warm.
I'd prefer to live in France (in Belgium, in Switzerland).
There are mountains and lakes.

Pour parler des fêtes ...

Quelle est la fête la plus importante pour ta famille?
Quelle fête préfères-tu?
Pour moi, la fête la plus importante, c'est mon anniversaire (Noël).
Parce que je sors avec mes amis.
A Noël, nous mangeons beaucoup et nous buvons trop.
Toute la famille est ensemble.

To talk about holidays and festivals ...

Which is the most important festival for your family?
Which festival do you prefer?
For me, the most important festival is my birthday (Christmas).
Because I go out with my friends.
At Christmas, we eat a lot and drink too much.
All the family is together.

Pour parler du temps ...

Quel temps fera-t-il demain?
D'après la météo, il y aura des nuages.
Le matin, il fera beau.
On dit qu'il y aura du brouillard (du vent).
On prévoit de la pluie et de la neige.
Dans la moitié nord du pays, il y aura des orages.

To talk about the weather ...

What will the weather be like tomorrow?
According to the weather forecast, it will be cloudy.
In the morning, it will be fine.
They say it will be foggy (windy).
They forecast rain and snow.
In the northern half of the country, there will be storms.

Vous faites un séjour chez un ami à Lille, une grande ville industrielle dans le nord de la France. Vous parlez de Lille et du petit village où vous vivez, au Pays de Galles.

1 Practise this conversation with a partner and learn all the girl's answers.

2 Take turns to put the boy's questions to each other and to answer them for yourselves.

Exam Practice

A

Look at the drawings and answer this question:
Quel temps est-ce qu'on prévoit pour demain?

Example:

Il y aura de la pluie.

1 **2** **3** **4** **5** **6**

B

Here are some questions your teacher could ask you on this topic. Answer each one and give a reason for each answer.

1 Que penses-tu de notre ville?

2 Quelle est la différence entre notre ville et Paris?

3 Que penses-tu du climat ici, en été?

4 Pour toi, quelle est la fête la plus importante?

5 Quel temps fera-t-il demain?

C

1 Revise carefully the phrases on pages 34, 36, 38 and 40. Get your partner to test you to make sure that you know them all and can spell all the words.

2 Cover the Teacher's Role and the Candidate's Answers below. Prepare the Candidate's Role and be ready to give more than one detail in each answer or to give a reason for your answer.

3 Now read the Teacher's Role and one candidate's answers.

4 Each answer at Higher Tier role play can score a maximum of four marks. Look at the marks this candidate scored. Explain why he/she lost marks (see page 29).

5 Re-write each answer to score the full four marks.

6 Practise the role-play with a partner and help each other to score full marks for every answer.

> ### Candidate's Role
>
> You are telling your French friend about your local area and a recent visit to a concert. Your teacher will play the part of your friend and will speak first.
> 1 Détails de la région.
> 2 Concert au théâtre.
> 3 Sorte de concert et opinion.
> 4 !

(AQA/NEAB – 1998)

> ### Teacher's Role
>
> 1 Qu'est-ce qu'il y a à faire, dans ta région? *(Candidate's task: to give three details about what there is to do.)*
> 2 Tu vas souvent au théâtre? *(Candidate's task: to say he/she went to a concert there.)*
> 3 C'était quelle sorte de concert et comment l'as-tu trouvé? *(Candidate's task: to say what sort of concert it was and give an opinion about it.)*
> 4 Comment es-tu rentré(e) à la maison, et à quelle heure? *(Candidate's task: to say how he/she arrived home and at what time.)*

> ### Candidate's Answers
>
> 1 Qu'est-ce qu'il y a à faire, dans ta région?
> – **On peut faire des promenades, on peut visiter le château.** (2 marks)
> 2 Tu vas souvent au théâtre?
> – **Oui, par exemple, j'ai été au théâtre la semaine dernière.** (2 marks)
> 3 C'était quelle sorte de concert et comment l'as-tu trouvé?
> – **Pop.** (0 marks)
> 4 Comment es-tu rentré(e) à la maison, et à quelle heure?
> – **Je suis rentré(e) à minuit.** (2 marks)

D

Imagine that you are staying in this village in the French Alps. Write a dialogue in which you compare this village with where you live.

Pour demander où c'est …
Pardon, monsieur (madame).
Où est l'arrêt d'autobus?
Il y a une station-service près d'ici?
Pour aller à la gare SNCF, s'il vous plaît?
La poste est près d'ici?

To ask where it is …
Excuse me.
Where is the bus stop?
Is there a petrol station near here?
How do I get to the railway station, please?
Is the post office near here?

Pour dire où c'est …
Prenez la première (deuxième) rue à gauche.
Allez tout droit.
Prenez la troisième rue à droite.
Aux feux, tournez à gauche.
Passez le pont.
L'hôtel est près de l'autoroute.
Le garage est en face de l'église.
C'est juste après l'aéroport.

To say where it is …
Take the first (second) street on the left.
Go straight on.
Take the third street on the right.
At the lights, turn left.
Cross the bridge.
The hotel is near the motorway.
The garage is opposite the church.
It's just after the airport.

C'est à quelle distance?
C'est loin d'ici?
C'est à dix minutes à pied (en voiture).
C'est à deux kilomètres environ.
C'est tout près d'ici.
On peut y aller à pied?
C'est trop loin.
Il faut prendre l'autobus.
Merci beaucoup.
Au revoir.

How far is it?
Is it far from here?
It's 10 minutes on foot (by car).
It's about two kilometres from here.
It's very close to here.
Can we walk there?
It's too far.
You have to take the bus.
Thank you very much.
Goodbye.

Ⓐ Vous êtes en France et vous voulez poster une carte postale.

1 Read Cartoon **Ⓐ**. Write it out in full, then practise it with a partner.
2 Now look at Cartoon **Ⓑ** and write the conversation in full.
3 Work with a partner. Make up two more dialogues by changing some details in
  Cartoon **Ⓑ**, e.g. *Pardon, monsieur. Pour aller à l'aéroport, s'il vous plaît?*

Ⓑ Vous êtes en France et vous voulez prendre un train pour aller à Paris.

Exam Practice

> ### Exam Tip
> In your exam, the topic of 'Finding the Way' will usually be combined with another topic. You need to practise combining topics to prepare for your exam. Before you do the tasks below, revise the topics on the right:
>
> - Free Time and Special Occasions: page 30
> - Leisure and Arranging to Meet: page 34
> - Home Town: page 40

A

1 Without looking at any of the lists, write the French for these tasks:
   a Ask where the post office is.
   b Say take the second street on the left.
   c Ask if there is a hotel nearby.
   d Say it is raining.
   e Ask if it is far.
   f Say you must take the bus.
   g Ask when you are going to the cinema.
   h Say it's about 10 minutes from here.
   i Say the cinema is opposite the bus stop.

Il y a un hôtel près d'ici?

 ## B

1 Prepare the role-play and practise it with a partner. Then write the dialogue in full.
2 Now change one detail in the dialogue and act it out again. Can your partner spot what you have changed?

Teacher's Role	Candidate's Role
Vous êtes en Suisse. Moi, je suis votre ami(e).	You are staying with a Swiss friend near Geneva and are planning to go out.
1 Tu veux sortir, ce matin?	1 Say the weather is nice.
2 Où veux-tu aller?	2 Say you would like to go to town.
3 Bonne idée!	3 Ask if it is far.
4 C'est à sept kilomètres environ.	4 Ask when you are going.
5 A dix heures.	Your teacher will play the part of your friend and will speak first.

 ## C

1 Cover the Teacher's Role and prepare the role-play. Try to guess what the teacher may ask for the ! and prepare good answers to these questions.
2 Look at the Teacher's Role and practise the role-play with a partner.

Teacher's Role	Candidate's Role
Vous êtes en France. Moi, je suis votre ami(e).	You are planning what to do today with your French friend.
1 Oh, regarde, il pleut!	1 Ask your friend what you are going to do this morning.
2 On peut aller au cinéma, si tu veux.	2 Ask if it is far.
3 C'est à vingt minutes d'ici.	3 Ask if you have to go by bus.
4 Oui, si tu veux. Et qu'est-ce que tu veux faire, ce soir?	4 !
5 Bonne idée!	Your teacher will play the part of your friend and will speak first.

Pour demander son chemin …

	To ask the way …

To ask the way …

Pour aller au syndicat d'initiative, s'il vous plaît? — How do I get to the tourist information office, please?
Vous allez jusqu'à l'hôpital, où vous tournez à droite. — You go as far as the hospital, where you turn right.
Vous descendez cette rue. — You go down this street.
Vous quittez l'autoroute à la prochaine sortie. — You leave the motorway at the next exit.
Il y a un parking à côté de la gare routière. — There is a car park next to the coach station.

A la station-service …
At the petrol station …

Le plein, s'il vous plaît. — Fill it up, please.
Trente litres d'ordinaire (de super). — 30 litres of premium (super).
Cent francs de sans plomb. — 100 francs worth of lead free.
Pouvez-vous vérifier l'huile (l'eau, les pneus)? — Can you check the oil (the water, the tyres)?
Vous avez une carte routière de la région? — Do you have a road map for the area?
La quatre, c'est combien, s'il vous plaît? — (Pump number) 4, how much is it please?

Quand vous tombez en panne …
When you break down …

Nous sommes en panne. — We've broken down.
Pouvez-vous envoyer quelqu'un? — Can you send someone?
Qu'est-ce qui ne va pas? — What's wrong?
Les freins ne marchent pas. — The brakes aren't working.
Le moteur ne marche pas. — The engine isn't working.
Je ne sais pas exactement. — I don't know exactly.
Où êtes-vous? — Where are you?
Je suis sur la Route Nationale 1, entre Boulogne et Calais. — I'm on the A road number 1, between Boulogne and Calais.
Nous sommes sur une petite route, au sud de Lille. — We're on a little road, south of Lille.
C'est quelle marque de voiture? — What make of car is it?
C'est une Ford blanche. — It's a white Ford.
Le numéro d'immatriculation, c'est T59 FRU. — The registration number is T59 FRU.
Le mécanicien sera là dans une demi-heure. — The mechanic will be there in half an hour.
J'attendrai dans la voiture. — I'll wait in the car.
Vous pouvez la réparer aujourd'hui? — Can you repair it today?
Mon bateau part à vingt et une heures. — My boat leaves at 9 p.m.

Vous allez à Paris en voiture, avec votre famille. Soudain, vous tombez en panne, dans un village.

1 Work with a partner to complete this conversation. Act it out and take turns to be the boy.
2 Write a different conversation based on the following instructions.
   You have broken down in France and you phone a garage.
   1 You are driving a blue Rover.
   2 Your brakes aren't working.
   3 You are on the A road between Avignon and Orange.
   4 The garage is two kilometres away.

Exam Practice

A

Make sure that you really know all the phrases on page 44. Cover them up and answer these questions. Remember to give two details or a reason in each answer.

1 You have broken down. Answer the mechanic's questions.

  a Où êtes-vous exactement?

  b Qu'est-ce qui ne va pas?

  c C'est quelle marque de voiture?

  d Quel est le numéro d'immatriculation?

2 You are walking to school and a French person asks you the way.

  a Il y a une station-service près d'ici?

  b C'est loin?

3 You go to a petrol station in France.

  a Vous voulez 40 l. de sans plomb.

  b Vous voulez aussi:

  c Vous demandez au pompiste de vérifier:

B

1 Each of these role-play instructions leads you to one of the phrases on page 44. Find the best phrase for each instruction and write it down.

  Example: a *Pour aller au syndicat d'initiative, s'il vous plaît?*

  a Vous voulez des renseignements.

  b Parking.

  c Pneus?

  d Problème?

  e Où?

  f Marque?

  g Couleur.

  h Numéro.

  i 100 F.

  j Huile?

  k Freins.

  l 30 m.

2 Now look again at page 44. Write out all the phrases which a garage mechanic would probably say when speaking to a motorist who has broken down.

C

1 Cover the Teacher's Role and prepare the Candidate's Role.

Teacher's Role	Candidate's Role
1 Allô, Garage Leclerc. Je peux vous aider? *(Candidate's task: to say what the problem is and what he/she wants.)* 2 Qu'est-ce qui ne va pas? *(Candidate's task: to explain exactly what is wrong.)* 3 Le mécanicien arrivera bientôt. Où êtes-vous exactement et c'est quelle marque de voiture? *(Candidate's task: to explain exactly where the car is and what make it is.)* 4 Où allez-vous attendre? *(Candidate's task: to say exactly where he/she will wait.)* 5 D'accord.	You are on the way to Calais to catch a 5 p.m. ferry. Your car breaks down on the motorway, 8 kms. south of Calais. You phone a garage for help. 1 Le problème. 2 Ce qui ne va pas. 3 Votre voiture. 4 ! Your teacher will play the part of the mechanic and will speak first.

(Adapted from AQA/NEAB – 1997)

2 Here are some possible answers. They are not in the correct order. Put them in the correct order and write the dialogue in full.

  – Nous sommes sur l'autoroute à huit kilomètres au sud de Calais. C'est une Peugeot verte.

  – Je ne sais pas exactement, mais le moteur ne marche pas.

  – J'attendrai dans la voiture, au bord de l'autoroute.

  – Nous sommes en panne. Pouvez-vous envoyer quelqu'un?

3 Practise the dialogue with a partner and learn it by heart.

4 Take turns to play the teacher's part, changing the order of the questions so that you practise answering them in any order.

Pour trouver un magasin …

Où est la boulangerie (la boucherie)?
Il y a un centre commercial près d'ici?
Où est-ce que je peux acheter des bananes?
La pâtisserie ouvre (ferme) à quelle heure?
L'épicerie est ouverte jusqu'à midi.

To find a shop …

Where is the baker's (the butcher's)?
Is there a shopping centre near here?
Where can I buy some bananas?
At what time does the cake shop open (close)?
The grocer's is open until midday.

Pour acheter des vêtements …

Je voudrais une chemise en coton.
Je voudrais une paire de baskets.
Pointure quarante-trois.
Avez-vous ce chemisier en rouge?
Quelle taille?
Grande (moyenne, petite).
C'est trop petit (large).
C'est combien?
Je cherche du parfum pour ma mère.
J'ai seulement cinquante francs (dix euros).

To buy clothes …

I'd like a cotton shirt.
I'd like a pair of trainers.
Size 43.
Have you got this blouse in red?
What size?
Large (medium, small).
It's too small (wide).
How much is it?
I'm looking for some perfume for my mother.
I've only got 50 francs (10 euros).

Pour acheter de quoi manger et boire …

Je voudrais un kilo de pommes.
Quatre tranches de jambon, s'il vous plaît.
Donnez-moi aussi une bouteille d'Orangina.
Je peux avoir une boîte d'abricots?
Il n'y a plus de framboises.
Avez-vous des fraises?
Et avec ça?
Ce sera tout, merci.

To buy food and drink …

I'd like a kilo of apples.
Four slices of ham, please.
Give me a bottle of Orangina as well.
Can I have a tin of apricots?
There are no raspberries left.
Have you got any strawberries?
Anything else?
That will be all, thanks.

Pour exprimer vos opinions …

Le pantalon n'est pas assez grand (long).
Cette robe est jolie (moche).
Je prends ce T-shirt.
C'est trop cher.
Je ne le prends pas.
Vous avez quelque chose de moins cher?
J'aime bien cet imperméable.
Je peux l'essayer (les essayer)?

To express your opinions …

The trousers aren't big (long) enough.
That dress is pretty (ugly).
I'll take this T-shirt.
It's too expensive.
I won't take it.
Do you have anything less expensive?
I quite like that raincoat.
Can I try it (them) on?

Vous allez au marché acheter des fruits pour un pique-nique.

(Adapted from AQA/NEAB – 1998)

1 Read the cartoon, then write it in full.
2 Learn the boy's part by heart. Then work in pairs: Partner A reads the part of the
   market vendor; Partner B covers the cartoon and says the boy's part, using these cues:

   1 Say hello to the lady.
   2 You would like four bananas.
   3 Ask if she has any strawberries.

   4 Say you would like a kilo of apples.
   5 You don't want anything else.

Exam Practice

 A

1 Work with a partner. Partner A says one of the sentences in the first box. Partner B
listens and says a sentence from the second box, and so on. See how many different
conversations you can make up.

2 Write two different conversations based on this.

A	B	A	B	A
Je voudrais un short en coton. Je voudrais une bouteille de limonade. Je voudrais un T-shirt en rouge. Je voudrais une paire de sandales.	Quelle taille? Quelle pointure? Grande ou petite?	Grande. Moyenne. Pointure quarante-cinq. Pointure trente-neuf.	Il n'y a plus rien dans cette taille. Je n'ai plus rien dans cette pointure. Je n'ai plus de limonade. Voilà, mademoiselle (monsieur).	Il y a un autre magasin près d'ici? D'accord, merci, au revoir. Merci, je les prends. Merci, je le prends. Avez-vous de l'Orangina?

 B

1 Cover the Teacher's Role and Model Answers, and prepare the role-play.

2 Uncover the Teacher's Role and work with a partner, taking turns to play both parts.

3 Uncover the Model Answers. Act the dialogue with a partner and learn your lines.

4 Cover the Model Answers again and write the dialogue in full.

Teacher's Role	**Candidate's Role**
Vous êtes dans un grand magasin, à Bordeaux. Moi, je suis le vendeur (la vendeuse). 1 Bonjour. Je peux vous aider? 2 Quelle taille? 3 De quelle couleur? 4 Voilà. 5 Deux cents francs.	You are in a department store in Bordeaux. 1 You would like to buy a pair of trousers. 2 You take a medium size. 3 You like the red trousers. 4 Ask how much they are. Your teacher will play the part of the shop assistant and will speak first.

Model Answers	*Exam Tip*
1 Je voudrais un pantalon. 2 Moyenne. 3 J'aime le pantalon rouge. 4 C'est combien?	When the instruction tells you to say **what you would like**, you must say *Je voudrais ...* When the instruction tells you to say **what you like**, you must say *J'aime ...*

 C

1 Cover the Teacher's Role and prepare this role-play in four minutes.

2 Look at the Teacher's Role and act the dialogue with a partner, taking turns to play
both roles.

Teacher's Role	**Candidate's Role**
Vous êtes en France. Moi, je suis le vendeur (la vendeuse). 1 Je peux vous aider? 2 Oui, prenez la première rue à gauche. Oui, vous désirez? 3 Quelle pointure et quelle couleur voulez-vous? 4 Voilà, vous les aimez? 5 Bien sûr.	You want to buy a pair of trainers. 1 Ask if there is a shopping centre nearby. 2 In the shop, say that you would like a pair of trainers. 3 ! 4 Ask if you can try them on. Your teacher will speak first.

Quand vous cherchez quelque chose …
Où est-ce que je pourrais acheter un bic (du parfum)?
Où est le rayon de vêtements?
Le rayon de disques est au rez-de-chaussée.
Le rayon parfumerie est au premier étage.

When you are looking for something …
Where could I buy a biro (some perfume)?
Where is the clothes department?
The record department is on the ground floor.
The perfume department is on the first floor.

Pour exprimer vos opinions …
Tu aimes faire les magasins?
Le samedi, je fais toujours les magasins.
Je ne fais jamais les magasins, je déteste ça.
Je préfère aller au supermarché parce qu'on y trouve de tout.

Les magasins sont fermés entre midi et une heure et demie.
Le dimanche, il y a moins de monde.

To express your opinions …
Do you like shopping?
On Saturdays, I always go shopping.
I never go shopping, I hate it.
I prefer going to the supermarket because you find everything there.
The shops are shut between midday and 1.30.
On Sundays, there aren't so many people.

Quand il y a un problème …
J'ai acheté cette montre (ce jean) ici, hier.
La radio ne marche pas.
La fermeture éclair est cassée.
Il y a un trou (une tache).
Je peux échanger ce pull-over?
Je l'ai acheté pour un ami mais il ne l'aime pas.
Pouvez-vous me le (la) remplacer?
Nous n'en avons plus.
Pourriez-vous me rembourser?
Voilà le reçu.
Ces chaussures sont trop chères.
Merci, mais je ne prends rien.
Passez à la caisse.

When there is a problem …
I bought this watch (these jeans) here, yesterday.
The radio does not work.
The zip is broken.
There is a hole (a mark).
Can I change this pullover?
I bought it for a friend, but he doesn't like it.
Can you replace it for me?
We don't have any left.
Could you give me my money back?
There's the receipt.
These shoes are too expensive.
Thank you, but I won't take anything.
Go to the cash desk.

Vous avez acheté un maillot de bain, hier. De retour à votre hôtel, vous voyez une tache sur le maillot. Vous retournez donc au magasin …

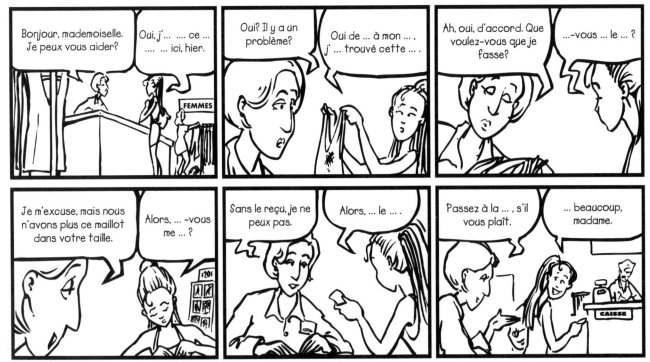

1 Read the cartoon and write the conversation in full.
2 Act it with a partner, taking turns to play each role: the customer should change one or two details each time (e.g. what you bought, what is wrong with it).

Exam Practice

A

1 Make sure that you really know all the phrases on pages 46 and 48. Ask your partner to test you.

2 The role-play instructions at Higher Tier usually leave you a lot of freedom. This means that you can often say what you are confident you know well. Look at the cues on the right and, for each one, write all the phrases from pages 46 and 48 which you could use.

3 Cover page 48 and what you have written. Look again at the cues and write as many sentences as you can think of to go with each one.

- Où?
- Objet.
- Problème.
- Détails du problème.
- Solution.
- Reçu.

Exam Tips
- Will you use *tu* or *vous* when you speak? Why?
- You have a lot of freedom in how you answer the questions, so use language that you know well. You will score higher marks and you won't waste time using a dictionary.

B

1 Looking only at the Candidate's Role, prepare the role-play in five minutes.

2 Work with a partner, taking turns to play the teacher's part.

Teacher's Role

1 Je peux vous aider? *(Candidate's task: to explain that he/she has a problem with the T-shirt.)*

2 Quel est le problème? *(Candidate's task: to say exactly what is wrong with the T-shirt.)*

3 Vous pouvez prouver que vous l'avez acheté ici? *(Candidate's task: to explain or offer proof of purchase.)*

4 Je m'excuse, mais nous n'avons plus de ces T-shirts. Que voulez-vous faire? *(Candidate's task: to make an alternative suggestion.)*

5 D'accord.

Candidate's Role

You are staying on holiday with a friend in France. You have bought a T-shirt as a present for your friend, but unfortunately you have to take it back to the shop.

1 Problème.
2 Détails du problème.
3 Reçu.
4 !

Your teacher will play the part of the shop assistant and will speak first.

(Adapted from AQA/NEAB – 1998)

C

1 Revise carefully all the phrases on pages 26 and 48.

2 Cover the Teacher's Role and prepare your role in six minutes.

3 Look at the Teacher's Role. Practise with a partner until you can both play the Candidate's Role perfectly.

4 With your partner, use the pictures of objects and problems to adapt the dialogue. Then write two new dialogues based on the pictures.

Teacher's Role

1 Je peux vous aider? *(Candidate's task: to say he/she wants to change the present.)*

2 Quel est le problème? *(Candidate's task: to give a reason for wanting to change it.)*

3 Pouvez-vous décrire le vendeur qui vous l'a vendu? *(Candidate's task: to describe the assistant who served him/her.)*

4 Oui, je sais qui c'est. Je m'excuse, mais nous n'avons plus exactement ce que vous avez acheté. *(Candidate's task: to offer an alternative suggestion.)*

5 D'accord.

Candidate's Role

You are in Belgium. You have bought a present for a friend. You go back to the department store to change it because there is a problem.

1 Problème.
2 Détails du problème.
3 Description du vendeur.
4 !

Your teacher will play the part of the shop assistant and will speak first.

(Adapted from AQA/NEAB – 1998)

Pour poster quelque chose ...

La poste est près d'ici?
Il y a un tabac près d'ici?
Où est la boîte aux lettres?
Je voudrais envoyer une lettre en Grande-Bretagne.
*C'est combien pour envoyer une carte postale en Angleterre
(au Pays de Galles)?*
Un timbre à trois francs vingt, s'il vous plaît.

To post something ...

Is the post office near here?
Is there a tobaconnist's near here?
Where is the letter box?
I'd like to send a letter to Great Britain.
How much is it to send a postcard to England
(to Wales)?
A 3 francs 20 stamp, please.

Quand vous voulez téléphoner ...

Y a-t-il un téléphone public près d'ici?
Quel est votre numéro de téléphone?
C'est le dix, quatorze, trente, cinquante-deux.
Vous connaissez l'indicatif?
Pour le Royaume-Uni c'est le zéro, zéro, quarante-quatre.
Allô, je peux parler à Madame Cros, s'il vous plaît?
Allô, je voudrais parler à Martin, s'il vous plaît.
Est-ce que Marie est là?

When you want to phone ...

Is there a public phone nearby?
What's your phone number?
It's 10 14 30 52.
Do you know the code?
For the UK it's 00 44.
Hello, can I please speak to Mrs Cros?
Hello, I'd like to speak to Martin, please.
Is Marie there?

Quand vous voulez laisser un message ...

Vous pouvez me passer Monsieur Dauvin?
C'est de la part de qui?
C'est de la part de Mademoiselle Leduc.
Il/Elle n'est pas là.
Voulez-vous laisser un message?
Je peux lui laisser un message?
Dites au directeur que Monsieur Arnaud a téléphoné.
Demandez à Madame Platel de me rappeler.
Vous pouvez me rappeler?
Vers quelle heure? Vers vingt-deux heures.
*Mon numéro de téléphone, c'est le zéro, quatre, soixante-sept, onze,
cinquante-huit, dix-neuf.*

When you want to leave a message ...

Can you put me through to Mr Dauvin?
Who's speaking?
It's Miss Leduc.
He/She isn't there.
Would you like to leave a message?
Can I leave him/her a message?
Tell the manager that Mr Arnaud called.
Ask Mrs Platel to call me back.
Can you call me back?
At about what time? At about 10 p.m.
My telephone number is 04 67 11 58 19.

A Vous êtes en vacances en France. Vous décidez de téléphoner à votre amie.

1 Write the conversation out correctly, then practise it with a partner.
2 Act it out again, this time giving **your own** name.

B Vous êtes à la poste, en Suisse.

1 Act the dialogue with a partner, taking turns to play each part.
2 With a partner, make a new dialogue by changing the words underlined.
3 Write a variation of the dialogue, changing the words underlined.

Exam Practice

 A

Work with a partner to develop this dialogue, then write it out in full.

Vous travaillez dans un bureau et vous répondez au téléphone.

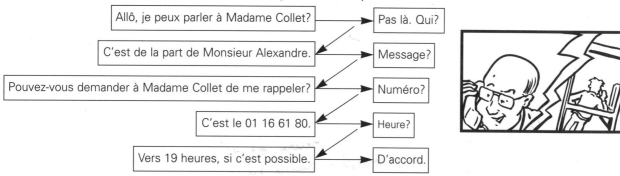

Allô, je peux parler à Madame Collet?	Pas là. Qui?
C'est de la part de Monsieur Alexandre.	Message?
Pouvez-vous demander à Madame Collet de me rappeler?	Numéro?
C'est le 01 16 61 80.	Heure?
Vers 19 heures, si c'est possible.	D'accord.

 B

1 Cover the Teacher's Role and Model Answers, and prepare the role-play.
2 Uncover the Teacher's Role and Model Answers, then practise with a friend until you are
   both perfect. Then write the dialogue in full.

Teacher's Role

Nous sommes dans un magasin, en France. Moi, je suis
le/la propriétaire.
1 Vous désirez?
2 C'est tout?
3 Oui, mais seulement pour les cartes postales.
4 Voilà, monsieur/mademoiselle.
5 Il y en a une à 200 mètres à gauche.

Candidate's Role

You are in a shop in France.
1 You want three postcards.
2 Ask if they sell stamps.
3 You want stamps for Great Britain.
4 Ask where the letter box is.

Your teacher will play the part of the shop assistant and
will speak first.

Model Answers

1 Je voudrais trois cartes postales.
2 Vous avez des timbres?
3 Je voudrais des timbres pour la Grande-Bretagne.
4 Où est la boîte aux lettres?

Exam Tip
Keep what you say short and simple. This reduces the risk of
mistakes.

 C

1 To prepare for the role-play, revise pages 12 and 50.
2 Cover the Teacher's Role and prepare your role.
3 With a partner, look at the Teacher's Role and take
   turns to play it. Practise till you're perfect!

Exam Tip
Role-plays in exams often combine language from two topics.
You need to be ready for this.

Teacher's Role

1 Allô, c'est Paul?
2 Paul est là, s'il vous plaît?
3 Pourquoi est-ce que vous ne faites pas les courses avec
   lui?
4 Je voudrais bien parler à Paul.
5 Après dix-neuf heures. Merci. Au revoir.

Candidate's Role

You are staying with your French friend, Paul. You answer
the telephone.
1 Say you are Paul's friend from Britain.
2 Say that Paul is shopping.
3 !
4 Ask when Paul can telephone the caller.

Your teacher will play the part of the caller and will speak
first.

(Adapted from AQA/NEAB – 1998)

<table>
<tr><td>

Quand vous allez à la poste …

Je voudrais envoyer ce paquet aux Etats-Unis (en Espagne).

C'est combien pour envoyer cette lettre en Allemagne (en France)?

Je peux envoyer cette lettre par avion?

C'est pour l'Autriche.

</td><td>

When you go to the post office …

I'd like to send this parcel to the USA (to Spain).

How much is it to send this letter to Germany (to France)?

Can I send this letter by airmail?

It's for Austria.

</td></tr>
<tr><td>

Quand vous changez de l'argent …

Je voudrais changer vingt livres sterling.

Je voudrais changer ces chèques de voyage.

Voilà mon passeport.

Vous pourriez me donner des billets de cent francs (dix euros)?

J'aimerais des pièces de cinquante centimes.

</td><td>

When you change money …

I'd like to change £20.

I'd like to change these traveller's cheques.

There's my passport.

Could you give me 100 franc (10 euro) notes?

I'd like some 50 centime coins.

</td></tr>
<tr><td>

Quand vous avez perdu quelque chose …

Où est le bureau des objets trouvés (le commissariat)?

J'ai perdu mon sac (mon portefeuille).

J'ai perdu mon appareil photo hier (ce matin).

Je l'ai laissé dans le métro (un taxi).

On m'a volé ma caméra vidéo.

Pouvez-vous décrire votre valise?

Elle est assez grande et noire.

Elle est en plastique (en cuir, en métal).

Elle est toute neuve.

Qu'est-ce qu'il y avait dedans?

Il y avait de l'argent et des clés.

C'est de quelle marque?

C'est une montre Tissot.

Je l'ai cherché(e) partout.

</td><td>

When you have lost something …

Where is the lost property office (the police station)?

I've lost my bag (my wallet).

I lost my camera yesterday (this morning).

I left it in the underground (a taxi).

Someone has stolen my video camera.

Can you describe your case?

It's quite big and black.

It's made of plastic (leather, metal).

It's brand new.

What was inside it?

There was some money and some keys.

What make is it?

It's a Tissot watch.

I've looked everywhere for it.

</td></tr>
<tr><td>

Quand vous voulez contacter quelqu'un …

Pourriez-vous m'envoyer un fax?

Je peux vous téléphoner (vous contacter par courrier électronique) demain?

Quel est votre numéro?

Une télécarte à cinquante unités, s'il vous plaît.

</td><td>

When you want to contact someone …

Could you send me a fax?

Can I phone you (contact you by E-mail) tomorrow?

What's your number?

A 50-unit phone card, please.

</td></tr>
</table>

Vous êtes en vacances, en Suisse. Un jour, vous entrez dans la chambre de votre hôtel et vous voyez que votre sac n'est plus là. Vous allez voir le directeur de l'hôtel.

(Adapted from AQA/NEAB – 1998)

1　Practise the conversation with a partner until you can both play both roles really well.

2　Partner A reads the hotel manager's part. Partner B covers the cartoon and plays the other part, using these instructions:

- Sac.
- Chambre.
- !
- Description.

Exam Practice

A

1 Write this dialogue in full. Remember what you must do to score four marks for each of your responses (see page 29).

You have lost your camera in Paris. You go to the lost property office.

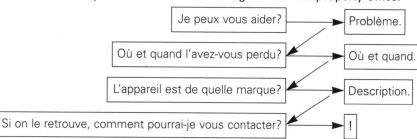

Je peux vous aider?	→	Problème.
Où et quand l'avez-vous perdu?	→	Où et quand.
L'appareil est de quelle marque?	→	Description.
Si on le retrouve, comment pourrai-je vous contacter?	→	!

2 The answers below all scored four marks. Write your own answers so that they will score four marks, and learn them.

a Oui, s'il vous plaît. J'ai perdu mon appareil photo.

b Je l'ai laissé dans le métro, ce matin.

c C'est un appareil Minolta. Il est tout neuf et il est dans un sac noir.

d Vous pouvez toujours m'envoyer un fax ou me téléphoner. Mon numéro, c'est le 0044 181 654321.

B

1 Look at page 52 and see how many answers you can find for each of these questions.

A la poste

Je peux vous aider?

Au bureau de change

Je peux vous aider?

Comment voulez-vous vos cent francs?

Au bureau des objets trouvés

Je peux vous aider?

Vous pouvez décrire votre valise?

Qu'est-ce qu'il y avait dedans?

Où l'avez-vous cherchée?

2 Cover page 52 and what you have just written. Give yourself 10 minutes to write at least two answers to each of the questions.

C

1 Cover the Teacher's Role and prepare your role.

2 Look at the Teacher's Role and practise with a partner, taking turns to play each role. Help each other to score four marks for each response.

> *Exam Tip*
> Always read your instructions carefully. Note which details are specified and which you **have** to give. And note where you are free to give your own details in words that you know.

Teacher's Role

1 Je peux vous aider?
   (Candidate's task: to state what he/she has lost.)
2 Vous pouvez me décrire la valise?
   (Candidate's task: to describe the case and contents with at least four details.)
3 Où et quand l'avez-vous perdue? *(Candidate's task: to say when and where he/she lost the case.)*
4 Quel est votre nom et comment pourrai-je vous contacter? *(Candidate's task: to give surname, spell it and say how he/she can be contacted.)*
5 D'accord.

Candidate's Role

You go to a lost property office in Belgium after losing your suitcase.
1 Objet.
2 Description et contenu.
3 Où et quand.
4 !

Your teacher will play the part of the clerk and will speak first.

(Adapted from AQA/NEAB – 1998)

3 Work with a partner. Take turns to be the clerk. Adapt the dialogue to talk about the following things you have lost:

Pour aller en ville …

On peut prendre le métro pour aller en ville?
Il y a un bus qui va à la gare routière?
Prenez le bus numéro quinze.
Où est l'arrêt d'autobus?
L'arrêt est tout près de la maison.
Normalement, ça prend vingt minutes.

For getting into town …

Can we take the underground to get into town?
Is there a bus which goes to the bus station?
Take bus number 15.
Where is the bus stop?
The stop is very close to the house.
It normally takes 20 minutes.

Pour aller plus loin …

Il y a un car qui va à Calais?
C'est quel bus pour aller à la plage?
Il y a un bus qui va à la gare SNCF?
Où sont les toilettes?
Il y a un train tous les combien?
Toutes les trente minutes.
C'est direct?
Non, il faut changer.
Où est le quai numéro quatre?

To go further …

Is there a coach which goes to Calais?
Which bus goes to the beach?
Is there a bus which goes to the railway station?
Where are the toilets?
How often is there a train?
Every 30 minutes.
Is it direct?
No, you have to change.
Where is platform 4?

Quand vous achetez vos billets …

Un aller-retour pour Lyon.
Un aller simple pour Marseille.
En deuxième classe.
Je voudrais partir demain matin (aujourd'hui, tout de suite).
Un carnet, s'il vous plaît.
Le train pour Londres part de quel quai?
Le train pour Lille part à quelle heure?
A quatorze heures trente.
C'est combien?

When you buy your tickets …

A return ticket to Lyon.
A single ticket to Marseille.
Second class.
I'd like to leave tomorrow morning (today, straight away).
A book of tickets, please (for the underground or buses).
Which platform does the London train leave from?
At what time does the train for Lille leave?
At 2.30 p.m.
How much is it?

Dans le train …

Pardon, cette place est occupée?
Non, elle est libre.
Votre billet, s'il vous plaît. Voilà mon billet.
J'ai perdu mon billet.
Ce train s'arrête à Bordeaux?

In the train …

Excuse me, is this seat taken?
No, it's free.
Your ticket, please. Here's my ticket.
I've lost my ticket.
Does this train stop at Bordeaux?

Vous êtes à la gare SNCF, à Paris. Vous voulez aller voir un ami, à Lyon.

1 Practise reading the cartoon with a partner, taking turns to play each part.
2 Write the conversation, replacing the words underlined with other words.

Exam Practice

 A

1 In your exam, you will have to ask at least one question. Look at these instructions. What question will you ask for each one?

a Ask if there is a bus to the railway station.

b Ask how often the bus goes.

c Ask where the bus stop is.

d Ask how much it costs.

e Ask if a seat is taken.

f Ask if this train stops at Marseille.

> *Exam Tip*
> Keep your questions short and simple, but make them **sound** like questions by raising your voice at the end.

2 Your French friend asks you some questions about how to get into town from your home. Write the answers. Then practise asking and anwering the questions with a partner.

a Il y a un bus qui va en ville?

b Où est l'arrêt?

c Ça prend combien de temps?

d Il y a un bus tous les combien?

e C'est direct?

f C'est combien, un aller simple?

F/H **B**

1 Revise carefully the phrases on page 54. Ask someone to test you.

2 Prepare the role-play in four minutes.

3 Look at the jumbled sentences on the right. Write them in the correct order to make a conversation to match the instructions.

4 Practise with a partner until you can both perform both roles perfectly.

Candidate's Role

You are at a railway station in France.
1 Ask for a return ticket to Paris.
2 Ask where you must change.
3 !
4 Ask where the platform is.

(Adapted from AQA/NEAB – 1997)

– Où est le quai numéro huit?

– C'est direct.

– Je peux vous aider?

– Quand voulez-vous partir?

– Où est-ce qu'il faut changer?

– Je voudrais partir tout de suite.

– Alors, c'est le quai numéro huit.

– Un aller-retour pour Paris, en deuxième classe.

– C'est par là, à droite.

 C

1 Give yourself four minutes to prepare the role-play.

2 Then complete the candidate's answers on the right, making sure you give all the information required.

3 Write the dialogue in full and practise it with a partner, taking turns to play each role.

Candidate's Role

You are at the railway station in Boulogne.
1 You would like a single ticket to Paris.
2 You want to leave tomorrow, at about 10 o'clock.
3 !
4 Ask if there is a reduction for students.

> *Exam Tips*
> • Remember to read the instructions carefully and also to listen carefully to your teacher's questions.
> • Then give **all** the information you are asked for.

Employé(e):	Je peux vous aider?
Vous:	Je voudrais un aller simple …
Employé(e):	Quand voulez-vous partir?
Vous:	Je voudrais partir demain …
Employé(e):	Alors, demain matin, il y a un train à neuf heures dix et un autre à onze heures quarante.
Vous:	Alors, je prends le train de …
Employé(e):	Alors, deux cent dix francs.
Vous:	Il y a une réduction …?
Employé(e):	Oui, si vous avez une carte d'étudiant.
Vous:	Voilà ma …

Quand vous voyagez …
Le prochain vol pour Toulouse part à quelle heure?
Je voudrais réserver une place dans un compartiment non-fumeur.
Je voudrais un billet classe touriste pour Edimbourg.
Il faut payer un supplément si on prend le TGV?

When you travel …
What time does the next flight for Toulouse leave?
I'd like to reserve a seat in a non-smoking compartment.
I'd like a tourist class ticket to Edinburgh.
Do you have to pay a supplement if you take the fast train?

Pour parler des voyages …
Tu aimes voyager en car?
Je n'aime pas prendre le bateau parce que je suis toujours malade.
Le train est plus rapide que le car.
En bus, c'est moins cher qu'en taxi.
Je préfère voyager en voiture parce que c'est plus pratique.
J'aimerais mieux y aller en avion.

To talk about journeys …
Do you like travelling by coach?
I don't like taking a boat because I'm always ill.
The train is faster than the coach.
It's cheaper by bus than by taxi.
I prefer to travel by car because it's more convenient.
I'd prefer to go there by plane.

En cas d'accident …
Il y a eu un accident.
Un car est entré en collision avec un camion.
La moto était arrêtée aux feux (au bord de la route).

La voiture allait très vite.
Le camion n'a pas pu s'arrêter.
Il pleuvait mais la visibilité était bonne.
Il y avait du brouillard et la visibilité était mauvaise.
Il faisait beau.
C'est sur l'autoroute A10, à cinq kilomètres au nord d'Orléans.
L'accident a eu lieu devant la gare, à Nice.
Il y a plusieurs blessés.
Un piéton (un cycliste) est gravement blessé.
Il faut appeler police-secours (les pompiers).
Pouvez-vous envoyer une ambulance?

In the event of an accident …
There has been an accident.
A coach has collided with a lorry.
The motorbike was stopped at the lights (on the side of the road).
The car was going very fast.
The lorry could not stop.
It was raining but there was good visibility.
It was foggy and visibility was bad.
The weather was fine.
It's on the A10 motorway, 5 kilometres north of Orléans.
The accident happened in front of the station, at Nice.
Several people are injured.
A pedestrian (a cyclist) is badly hurt.
We must call the emergency service (the fire brigade).
Can you send an ambulance?

Vous allez en voiture avec votre famille sur la Côte d'Azur. Soudain, devant vous, il y a un accident. Vous téléphonez tout de suite à police-secours.

1 Practise the conversation with a partner, then make a new conversation by changing the underlined words.

2 Now adapt the conversation to match the instructions on the right, and write it in full.

There has been an accident on the A7 motorway, 30 kilometres north of Marseille. A coach has collided with a car and there are several injured people. The weather was fine and visibility was good, but the coach was going very fast, the car was stopped on the side of the road and the coach could not stop.

Exam Practice

A

1 Complete the two dialogues below by choosing the best answer for each gap from those in the box. Then practise the completed dialogues with your partner.

2 Partner A reads the questions. Partner B closes the book and makes up a new answer to each question. Then change roles.

A la gare SNCF	Une enquête dans la rue
Je peux vous aider?	Quand vous partez en voyage, quel moyen de transport préférez-vous?
....	
Le prochain TGV part demain matin, à neuf heures vingt. Vous voulez réserver une place?	....
	Y a-t-il un moyen de transport que vous n'aimez pas?
....	
Quelle classe?	....
	Quels sont les avantages du car sur le train?
....	
Non, il n'y a pas de supplément.	....
	Si vous alliez en Espagne, quel serait votre moyen de transport préféré?
....	
Cinq cents francs quarante.	....

a Le car est moins cher que le train mais il est moins rapide aussi.

b Le prochain TGV pour Montpellier part à quelle heure?

c En deuxième classe. Il faut payer un supplément si on prend le TGV?

d Normalement, je préfère le train parce que c'est rapide, confortable et pas cher.

e Oui, je voudrais réserver une place dans un compartiment non-fumeur.

f Oui, je déteste prendre le bateau parce que je suis toujours malade.

g J'aimerais mieux y aller en avion parce que ce serait rapide et pratique.

h Alors, c'est combien?

B

1 Use this flowchart to make up as many different conversations as you can.

2 Work on it with a partner and take turns to be the police officer.

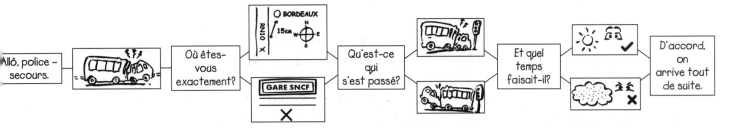

C

1 Cover the Teacher's Role and prepare your role.

2 Look at the Teacher's Role and practise with a partner.

> **Exam Tip**
> To prepare for this role-play, revise pages 18, 20 and 56.

Teacher's Role

1 Alors, qu'est-ce qui ne va pas? *(Candidate's task: to describe his/her symptoms, giving two details.)*

2 Alors, qu'est-ce qui s'est passé? *(Candidate's task: to say he/she has had an accident.)*

3 L'accident a eu lieu où et quand? *(Candidate's task: to say where and when it happened.)*

4 Je dois contacter quelqu'un. Vous avez un numéro de téléphone? *(Candidate's task: to say who can be contacted and give a telephone number.)*

5 D'accord, je téléphone tout de suite.

Candidate's Role

You have had an accident while in France and go to the hospital.

1 Symptômes.

2 Accident.

3 Où et quand.

4 !

Your teacher will play the part of the doctor and will speak first.

(Adapted from AQA/NEAB – 1997)

Pour parler de votre avenir …

Qu'est-ce que tu espères faire, après les examens?
J'espère rester au collège. Je voudrais aller au lycée.
Je vais quitter le collège.
Je voudrais faire histoire, anglais et géographie.
Qu'est-ce que tu veux faire plus tard?
Je veux être professeur (secrétaire).
Je voudrais bien commencer à travailler.

To talk about your future …

What do you hope to do, after the exams?
I hope to stay at school. I'd like to go to 6th form college.
I'm going to leave school.
I'd like to do history, English and geography.
What do you want to do later?
I want to be a teacher (secretary).
I'd really like to start to work.

Pour parler du travail …

Tu as déjà travaillé?
J'ai fait un stage en entreprise dans un hôtel.
J'ai travaillé dans un grand magasin pendant une semaine.
Qu'est-ce que tu fais comme travail?
Je travaille le week-end dans une station-service.
Je distribue des journaux tous les matins.
J'ai souvent fait du baby-sitting.
Tu gagnes combien?
On me paie quatre livres par heure.
J'aime bien mon job. Je n'aime pas le travail.
C'est intéressant (dur, ennuyeux).
Tu as un job?

To talk about work …

Have you already worked?
I've done a work experience in a hotel.
I've worked in a department store for a week.
What sort of work do you do?
At the weekend, I work in a petrol station.
I deliver newspapers every morning.
I've often done baby-sitting.
How much do you earn?
I get paid £4 an hour.
I really like my job. I don't like work.
It's interesting (hard, boring).
Do you have a job?

Pour parler de votre famille …

Ton père, qu'est-ce qu'il fait dans la vie?
Il est électricien (serveur, fermier).
Il travaille dans une usine (un bureau).
Ma mère est coiffeuse (infirmière, serveuse).
Mon frère est au chômage.
Ma sœur veut être informaticienne (vendeuse).

To talk about your family …

What does your dad do for a living?
He's an electrician (waiter, farmer).
He works in a factory (an office).
My mother is a hairdresser (nurse, waitress).
My brother is unemployed.
My sister wants to be a computer operator (shop assistant).

Vous êtes chez votre ami, au Québec, et vous parlez de votre job.

(Adapted from AQA/NEAB – 1998)

1 Practise the conversation with a partner.

2 Partner A reads the girl's part. Partner B covers the cartoon and plays the other part, using these pictures as cues:

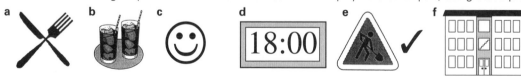

3 Now write a similar conversation, based on these pictures:

Exam Practice

 A

1 Cover the gapped dialogue on the right and prepare the role-play.

2 Uncover the dialogue and write it in full.

3 Practise with a partner until you are both word perfect.

Candidate's Role

You are talking to your Swiss friend about your part–time job.

1 You work in the kitchen of a restaurant.

2 You do the washing-up.

3 You earn £3 an hour.

4 You buy records and magazines.

Exam Tip

• Be very careful to pronounce your verbs correctly. You **must not** pronounce the *e* at the end of *je travaille, je gagne, j'achète.*

Tu parles avec ton ami(e) suisse. Moi, je suis ton ami(e).

– T... a... u... j... ?

– **O..., j... t... d... la c... d'un r... .**

– Q... fais-tu?

– **J... f... la v... .**

– T... g... c... ?

– **J... g... t... l... p... h... .**

– Q... fais-tu avec ton a... ?

– **J'... d... d... et d... m... .**

(Adapted from AQA/NEAB – 1998)

F/H **B**

1 Cover the French sentences on the right, and prepare the role-plays in eight minutes.

2 Write the sentences in the correct order to make up the two role-plays.

3 Practise with your partner until you are perfect.

Candidate's Role

Your French friend has just got a holiday job.

1 Ask what the job is.

2 Find out how many hours a day he/she works.

3 Find out how much he/she earns.

4 !

Your teacher will play the part of your friend and will speak first.

– Je suis serveur/serveuse dans un café.

– Je gagne deux mille francs par semaine.

– Oui, je travaille dans un grand magasin.

– Je commence à 9 heures et je finis à 15 heures.

– J'ai trouvé un job pour l'été.

– Toi aussi, tu as un job?

– Tu travailles combien d'heures par jour?

– Tu gagnes combien?

– Qu'est-ce que tu fais comme travail?

Candidate's Role

You are talking to your Belgian friend about finding a summer job.

1 Say you want to earn some money.

2 You would like to work in a restaurant.

3 You worked as a waiter/waitress last summer.

4 !

– Qu'est-ce que tu vas faire pendant l'été?

– Je voudrais travailler dans un restaurant.

– Oui, j'ai travaillé comme serveur/serveuse l'été dernier.

– J'espère aller en vacances avec des amis.

– Tu as déjà travaillé?

– Qu'est-ce que tu veux faire?

– Pourquoi veux-tu gagner de l'argent?

– Je veux gagner de l'argent.

(Adapted from AQA/NEAB – 1998) (Adapted from AQA/NEAB – 1997)

F/H **C**

1 Cover the Teacher's Role and prepare your role.

2 Look at the Teacher's Role and practise with a partner. Help each other to score three marks for each task.

Exam Tip

• Try to use a verb in each task.

• Make sure you pronounce the verbs correctly.

Teacher's Role

1 Voici une photo de mon frère.

2 Il est infirmier dans un grand hôpital.

3 Huit heures par jour. Et ton frère, que fait-il?

4 Et qu'est-ce que tu voudrais faire dans la vie?

5 C'est intéressant, ça.

The teacher plays the part of the friend and speaks first.

Candidate's Role

You and your friend from Sénégal are talking about your families.

1 Ask what your friend's brother does for a living.

2 Ask how long he works each day.

3 Say what your brother does.

4 !

The World of Work

Pour parler de votre éducation à l'avenir et dans le passé …	To talk about your education in the future and in the past …
Comment as-tu trouvé le collège?	How did you find school?
La plupart du temps, c'était très bien.	Most of the time it was very good.
J'ai beaucoup aimé les langues (les sciences).	I liked languages (science) very much.
Que penses-tu faire à l'avenir?	What are you thinking of doing in the future?
Si j'ai de bons résultats, j'irai à l'université.	If I get good results, I'll go to university.
Je voudrais étudier l'anglais (les maths).	I'd like to study English (maths).
Pourquoi veux-tu étudier le français (la médecine)?	Why do you want to study French (medicine)?
Parce que j'espère être professeur (dentiste).	Because I hope to be a teacher (dentist).
Je ne sais pas ce que je veux faire.	I don't know what I want to do.

Quand vous cherchez un emploi …	When you are looking for a job …
J'aimerais bien travailler dans une banque (un garage).	I'd really like to work in a bank (a garage).
Avez-vous un poste vacant?	Have you got a vacancy?
J'ai vu votre annonce sur le journal (dans la vitrine).	I saw your advert in the newspaper (in the window).
Je peux travailler tous les week-ends.	I can work every weekend.
Je serai libre à partir du début de juillet.	I will be free from the beginning of July.
Je suis libre jusqu'à la fin d'août.	I'm free until the end of August.
Je cherche un emploi à plein temps (à temps partiel).	I'm looking for a full-time (part-time) job.
Pouvez-vous m'envoyer des renseignements sur l'emploi?	Can you send me some information about the job?
Voulez-vous que je vous envoie mon curriculum-vitae?	Would you like me to send my CV?
Je travaillerais combien d'heures par jour?	How many hours a day would I work?
Je gagnerais combien par heure?	How much would I earn per hour?

Pour parler des avantages et des inconvénients …	To talk about the advantages and disadvantages …
L'avantage, c'est que les journalistes sont bien payés.	The advantage is that journalists are well paid.
L'inconvénient, c'est qu'un médecin doit souvent travailler la nuit.	The disadvantage is that a doctor often has to work at night.
Je ne voudrais pas travailler dans un bureau.	I would not like to work in an office.
Ce serait intéressant (facile, ennuyeux).	It would be interesting (easy, boring).

Vous cherchez un emploi, en France. Vous allez à une agence.

1 Practise the conversation with a partner.
2 Partner A reads the clerk's part. Partner B covers the cartoon and uses these cues to play the young man:
   • Sorte de travail. • Quand? • Expérience. • !

60

Exam Practice

A

1 Make sure you know all the phrases on pages 58 and 60, then study these role-play instructions and answer the questions about them.

Candidate's Role

You have seen an advertisement for a job as a waiter/waitress on the door of a café. You are very interested in the job and go in to make enquiries.

1 Emploi.
2 Raison.
3 Heures et salaire.
4 !
5 Dates.

Your teacher will play the part of the café owner.

2 Now link each of these instructions to the correct candidate's task:

  a To say when he/she is available for work, giving a starting date and a finishing date.

  b To explain that he/she is enquiring about the job advertised.

  c To ask what the hours and wages are.

  d To say why.

  e To explain what experience he/she has.

a Which tasks require you to use the information specified in the introduction?

b Which tasks require you to give an explanation?

c Which tasks leave you free to say what you want?

d How many details do you need to give for each task?

Exam Tip

When preparing a role-play, always look for:

– tasks defined for you in the introduction;

– tasks where you are free to say what you want;

– tasks where you may need to explain or justify something;

– how many details you need to give (aim to give at least two).

3 Here is the Teacher's Role. Work on the role-play with a partner until you can both perform it well.

Teacher's Role

1 Je peux vous aider?
2 Pourquoi voulez-vous cet emploi?
3 Vous avez des questions pour moi?
4 Il faudrait travailler quatre heures par jour, le samedi et le dimanche. Vous gagneriez 50 francs par heure. Vous avez déjà travaillé comme serveur/ serveuse?
5 Quand êtes-vous libre?
6 D'accord, je vous offre le poste.

(Adapted from AQA/NEAB – 1998)

B

1 Cover the Teacher's Role and prepare your role. Remember the Exam Tip above.

2 Read the questions your teacher will ask you. Write the conversation in full.

Teacher's Role

1 Il est difficile de trouver un bon job.
2 Tu travailles quand?
3 Que fais-tu?
4 Quels sont les avantages de ton job?
5 Tu as un bon job.

Candidate's Role

You are talking to your French friend about your part-time job and about work in general.

1 Lieu de travail.
2 Heures et jours.
3 Détails du travail.
4 !

3 Below is an example of one candidate's answers. Read the answers, and the notes which show what you must do to score full marks. Where has this candidate lost marks? Then write the conversation so that all the answers gain the full four marks.

Teacher: Il est difficile de trouver un bon job.

Candidate: Moi, j'ai un job. (*Task: To say where he/she works.*)

Teacher: Tu travailles quand?

Candidate: Je travaille le samedi. (*Task: To give hours and days of employment.*)

Teacher: Que fais-tu?

Candidate: Je sers les clients. (*Task: To give two details about his/her job.*)

Teacher: Quels sont les avantages de ton job?

Candidate: C'est assez bien payé. (*Task: To give two advantages of his/her job.*)

Teacher: Tu as un bon job.

Pour parler de vos vacances …

Que fais-tu pendant les vacances?
D'habitude, nous restons à la maison.
Où allez-vous en vacances?
Nous allons souvent au bord de la mer.
D'habitude, en été, nous allons à l'étranger.
Comment voyagez-vous?
Nous prenons la voiture (l'avion).
Avec qui vas-tu en vacances?
Je vais en vacances avec mes parents.
Vous partez pour combien de temps?
Nous partons toujours pour quinze jours.
Vous allez à l'hôtel?
Nous faisons du camping. Nous louons une maison.
Que faites-vous, le soir?
Le soir, on va en discothèque.
On va nager.

To talk about your holidays …

What do you do in the holidays?
We usually stay at home.
Where do you go for your holidays?
We often go to the seaside.
Usually, in summer, we go abroad.
How do you travel?
We take the car (the plane).
Who do you go on holiday with?
I go on holiday with my parents.
How long do you go for?
We always go for two weeks.
Do you go to a hotel?
We go camping. We rent a house.
What do you do in the evenings?
In the evenings we go to the disco.
We go swimming.

Pour parler de l'année dernière …

Où as-tu été, l'année dernière?
L'été dernier, j'ai été en France.
Comment as-tu voyagé? Nous avons pris le train.
Tu es parti(e) avec qui? Avec des amis.
Vous y avez passé combien de temps?
Nous avons passé huit jours à Cannes.
Nous avons loué un appartement. Nous avons fait du camping.
Qu'est-ce que (tu as) vous avez fait?
J'ai fait du ski.
On a joué sur la plage. On a fait des excursions.
Nous avons vu des choses intéressantes.
Quel temps a-t-il fait? Il a fait beau (mauvais).

To talk about last year …

Where did you go last year?
Last summer, I went to France.
How did you travel? We went by train.
Who did you go with? With some friends.
How long did you spend there?
We spent a week at Cannes.
We rented a flat. We went camping.
What did you do?
I went skiing.
We played on the beach. We did some excursions.
We saw some interesting things.
What was the weather like? The weather was good (bad).

Pour exprimer vos opinions …

Qu'est-ce que tu aimes faire en vacances?
J'aime aller au bord de la mer.
C'était formidable (intéressant, ennuyeux).
C'est amusant.

To express your opinions …

What do you like to do on holiday?
I like to go to the seaside.
It was great (interesting, boring).
It's fun.

Vous parlez des vacances avec votre ami(e).

1 Practise this with a partner, taking turns to play each part.
2 Write a new conversation. This time, the boy often goes to the seaside, plays on the beach and goes to discos.
3 Adapt the answers to say what **you** usually do on holiday. Then change the conversation to talk about what you did last year. You will need to change the questions, e.g. *Où as-tu été, l'été dernier?*

Exam Practice

 A

In your exam, you will have to ask at least one question. Ask these questions in French:

a Ask what your friend does in the holidays.

b Ask where they go.

c Ask how they travel.

d Ask who your friend goes on holiday with.

e Ask how long they go for.

f Ask what they do in the evenings.

g Ask where your friend went last year.

h Ask how he/she travelled.

i Ask who he/she went with.

j Ask what the weather was like.

k Ask what your friend did in the evenings.

> ### Exam Tips
> You must pronounce the verbs correctly or you will lose marks.
> So:
> - do **not** pronounce the last two letters of *tu aimes* (it sounds like 'emm');
> - do **not** pronounce the last letter of *tu fais* (it sounds like 'fay').

 B

1 Cover the gapped dialogue on the right and prepare your role in three minutes.

2 Look at the dialogue and write it in full.

3 Practise with a partner until you are both word perfect.

Candidate's Role

You are discussing holidays with your French friend.
1 Tell him/her you went skiing last year.
2 !
3 Tell him/her you usually go to the seaside in the summer.
4 Tell him/her what you do there.

When you see this – ! – you will have to respond to something which you have not prepared.

(AQA/NEAB – 1998)

– Où as-tu passé les vacances, l'hiver dernier?
– **J'... f... d... s... l'... d... .**
– Que penses-tu du ski?
– **C'... f... .**
– Que fais-tu d'habitude en été?
– **D'... , j... v... a... b... d... l... m... .**
– Et que fais-tu?
– **J... v... n... et j... v... e... d... .**
– Moi aussi, j'aime ça.

 C

Give yourself three minutes to prepare this role-play. Then practise it with a partner, taking turns to ask and answer the questions.

Teacher's Role

1 Salut! Je suis content(e) de te revoir.
2 J'ai été à la montagne, avec des amis.
3 Il a fait assez beau.
4 J'ai fait des promenades. Et toi, tu préfères quelle sorte de vacances, et pourquoi?

Candidate's Role

You are talking to your French friend about holidays.
1 Ask where your friend went last year.
2 Ask what the weather was like.
3 Ask what your friend did in the evenings.
4 !

Your teacher plays the part of the friend and speaks first.

(Adapted from AQA/NEAB – 1998)

D

L'été dernier, vous avez passé vos vacances ici.
Regardez la photo et répondez aux questions.

a Où as-tu été, l'année dernière?

b Comment as-tu voyagé?

c Tu es parti(e) avec qui?

d Tu y as passé combien de temps?

e Tu as été à l'hôtel?

f Qu'est-ce que tu as fait?

g Quel temps a-t-il fait?

Au syndicat d'initiative …

Vous avez un dépliant sur les châteaux de la Loire?
Nous voudrions louer un gîte.
Je voudrais faire l'excursion dans les Pyrénées.
L'autocar part d'où?

Pour exprimer vos préférences …

Où allons-nous en vacances, cet hiver?
J'aimerais aller dans une grande ville.
Moi, j'aimerais mieux aller faire du ski.
Je n'ai jamais été aux Etats-Unis.
Allons en Espagne!
J'ai déjà été en Italie. Ce n'était pas fantastique.
Je m'intéresse à l'art.
Y a-t-il un musée en ville?
J'aimerais surtout visiter la cathédrale.
Ce serait super!
Je ne voudrais pas faire de la voile: c'est dangereux et je ne nage pas bien.
J'aimerais mieux aller à l'hôtel parce qu'il pleut souvent là-bas.

Pour parler de vos vacances …

Mes vacances en Grèce étaient fantastiques parce qu'il y a fait si beau.
Il faisait trop chaud pour moi en Afrique.
Nous avons visité les ruines mais nous étions plutôt déçus.
Il y avait des touristes partout.
Où irez-vous, l'année prochaine?
J'aimerais bien aller en Autriche.
Nous préférons rester en Angleterre parce qu'on mange mieux ici.

In the tourist office …

Have you got a brochure on the castles of the Loire?
We'd like to rent a holiday home.
I'd like to do the excursion in the Pyrenees.
Where does the coach leave from?

To express your preferences …

Where shall we go on holiday this winter?
I'd like to go to a city.
Well, I'd prefer to go skiing.
I've never been to the USA.
Let's go to Spain!
I've already been to Italy. It wasn't fantastic.
I'm interested in art.
Is there a museum in town?
Above all, I'd like to visit the cathedral.
That would be great!
I wouldn't like to go sailing: it's dangerous and I can't swim well.
I'd prefer to go to a hotel because it often rains there.

To talk about your holidays …

My holidays in Greece were fantastic because the weather there was so good.
It was too hot for me in Africa.
We visited the ruins but we were rather disappointed.
There were tourists everywhere.
Where will you go next year?
I'd really like to go to Austria.
We prefer to stay in England because you eat better here.

L'année dernière, vous avez fait du camping près de Nice, sur la Côte d'Azur, en France. C'est une belle région avec des plages fantastiques. Votre ami belge vous parle de ces vacances.

(Adapted from AQA/NEAB – 1997)

1 Practise the conversation with a partner until you can reproduce it using only these cue words: *où, pourquoi, avec qui, bien, inconvénients, l'année prochaine.*

2 Now answer the same questions, but give your own answers.

Exam Practice

Exam Tips

- When you see this – ! – you know it will be difficult to prepare what to say. You can use the situation to guess, but you must listen carefully to the teacher's question and be flexible enough to answer it. In fact, this is also true for the other short cues – so listen carefully as the questions may not be quite what you expected!

- In this topic, you must be ready to discuss different types of holiday and to decide which holiday to choose. Your teacher may not agree with what you choose, so be ready to negotiate and persuade. Always give a reason for your choice, and always prepare an alternative, with a reason,.

A

1 Cover the Teacher's Role and prepare your role.

(Adapted from AQA/NEAB – 1998)

Teacher's Role	**Candidate's Role**
1 Allô.	You are telephoning your French friend to suggest a shopping trip to Paris.
2 Quand veux-tu y aller et comment veux-tu voyager?	1 Où et raison.
3 Je déteste faire les magasins. Il n'y a rien de plus intéressant à faire à Paris?	2 Comment et quand.
4 D'accord. On se voit où et quand?	3 !
5 D'accord. A bientôt.	4 Détails du rendez-vous.

2 Uncover the Teacher's Role and practise with a partner.

3 When you can both play this role well, Partner A asks the questions, but in a different order. This helps Partner B to practise listening carefully to the questions.

B

In your Higher Tier role-play, you usually have to state an opinion. Make sure that you then give a reason to justify the opinion. Complete the sentences below by adding a reason.

Example: *Nous voudrions louer un gîte parce que c'est intéressant et pas cher.*

a J'aimerais aller dans une grande ville, parce que …

b J'aimerais mieux visiter les musées, parce que …

c Je ne voudrais pas aller skier, parce que …

d J'aimerais mieux faire du camping, parce que …

C

1 Prepare this role-play in five minutes.

2 Now read the Teacher's Role and write out the whole conversation.

Candidate's Role

You and your Belgian friend are saving for a holiday together. You have reduced the choice to the two below.

Les Pyrénées	La Côte d'Azur
Camping	Hôtel
Montagnes	Plages + Soleil
Tranquille	Discothèques
Promenades	Voile
10 jours 950 francs	8 jours 1400 francs

1 Opinion.
2 !
3 Argent.
4 Dates des vacances.

Teacher's Role

1 Moi, je ne peux pas décider. Qu'est-ce que tu préfères, toi, et pourquoi?
  (Candidate's task: to state the preference and reason.)
2 *If the candidate chooses the Pyrenees, the teacher says:* Moi, j'aimerais mieux aller sur la Côte d'Azur. Tu aimes faire de la voile? *If the candidate chooses the French Riviera, the teacher says:* Moi, j'aimerais mieux aller dans les Pyrénées. Tu aimes faire des promenades?
  (Candidate's task: to express an opinion about the activity mentioned.)
3 Tu as raison. Comment vas-tu faire des économies pour payer les vacances? *(Candidate's task: to explain how the money for the holiday will be saved.)*
4 Les grandes vacances commencent et finissent quand? *(Candidate's task: to give details of holiday dates.)*
5 Très bien. Alors, je vais réserver les vacances.

(Adapted from AQA/NEAB – 1998)

Pour réserver une chambre ... / To reserve a room ...

Pour réserver une chambre ...	To reserve a room ...
Je voudrais réserver une chambre pour la nuit du premier février.	I'd like to reserve a room for the night of the 1st of February.
Je vous téléphone de l'Angleterre.	I'm phoning you from England.
Vous avez une chambre libre?	Do you have a room free?
Vous êtes combien? Nous sommes cinq.	How many of you are there? There are five of us.
Vous voulez quelle sorte de chambre?	What sort of room do you want?
Je voudrais une chambre pour une personne (deux personnes).	I'd like a single (double) room.
Avez-vous une chambre avec douche (salle de bains)?	Have you got a room with a shower (bathroom)?
C'est pour combien de nuits? C'est pour une nuit.	How many nights is it for? It's for one night.
C'est combien par personne (par nuit)?	How much is it per person (per night)?
Je prends cette chambre.	I'll take that room.
Je regrette, mais l'hôtel est complet.	I'm sorry, but the hotel is full.
Je peux venir dans quinze jours?	Can I come in two weeks?
Il y a un autre hôtel près d'ici?	Is there another hotel nearby?

Quand vous arrivez à l'hôtel ... / When you arrive at the hotel ...

Quand vous arrivez à l'hôtel ...	When you arrive at the hotel ...
J'ai réservé une chambre pour cette nuit.	I've reserved a room for tonight.
J'ai réservé une chambre à deux lits (avec un grand lit).	I reserved a room with two beds (with a double bed).
C'est au nom de Jones.	It's in the name of Jones.
Où est le restaurant (le parking)?	Where is the restaurant (the car park)?
Où sont les toilettes?	Where are the toilets?
Le petit déjeuner est compris?	Is breakfast included?
Le petit déjeuner est à quelle heure?	At what time is breakfast?
La pension complète, c'est combien?	How much is full board?
Je peux avoir ma clé, s'il vous plaît, chambre cent dix?	May I have my key, please, room 110?
Je peux avoir ma note, s'il vous plaît?	May I have my bill, please?

Vous allez à un hôtel à Strasbourg, dans l'est de la France.

(Adapted from AQA/NEAB – 1998)

1 Practise this conversation with a partner and learn the boy's lines.
2 Cover the cartoon and write the conversation below in full.
3 Check with the cartoon that you have written the conversation correctly.

Réceptionniste	Client
– Bonjour, monsieur.	– (You want to book a single room.)
– C'est pour combien de nuits?	– (You want to stay for two nights.)
– D'accord, chambre cent vingt.	– (Ask if the room has a shower or a bath.)
– Toutes nos chambres sont avec salle de bains.	– (Ask how much it costs.)
– Trois cents francs.	– (Ask if breakfast is included.)
– Non, monsieur, le petit déjeuner coûte quarante francs.	– (Say you will have the room.)

Exam Practice

F **A**

1 Make sure that you have learnt all the phrases on page 66. Ask a partner to test you.

2 Complete the conversation below in French, and write it in full.

3 Practise it with a partner until you are both perfect.

> **Exam Tip**
> Keep your answers short and simple.

Vous allez à l'hôtel, en France.

Je peux vous aider?	You want a room for one night.
Vous voulez quelle sorte de chambre?	You would like a single room.
Oui, j'ai une belle chambre.	Ask if the room has a bathroom.
Oui, toutes nos chambres ont une salle de bains.	Ask how much the room costs per night.
Quatre cents francs, avec le petit déjeuner.	Say you will take the room.

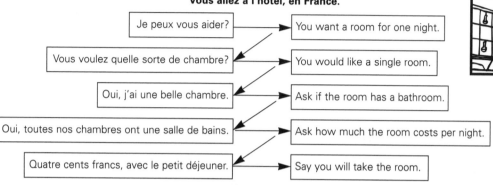

F **B**

1 Write a French sentence to go with each symbol.

Example: *Je voudrais une chambre pour une personne.*

a  ? **b** 2×   **c** ? **d**   **e** P ? **f** ? **g** ?

2 Write a conversation using all these sentences and including what the receptionist says.

3 Practise in pairs: one plays the receptionist and the other the client.

F/H **C**

1 Cover the Teacher's Role and, in three minutes only, prepare the Candidate's Role.

2 Look at the Teacher's Role and practise the conversation with a partner. Continue until you can both play the client's part perfectly.

> **Exam Tips**
> • Always read the instructions very carefully and prepare exactly what they tell you.
> • Do not use a dictionary. If you learn the phrases in this book, you won't need the dictionary. Then you will do your role-plays faster and better!
> • You must give a reason for changing your reservation. Keep this simple and say something you know, e.g. *Je suis malade. J'ai eu un accident.*

Teacher's Role

1 Allô, Hôtel du Parc.
2 Oui, et votre réservation est pour quand?
3 Il y a un problème?
4 Pourquoi exactement?
5 D'accord.

Candidate's Role

You telephone a French hotel.
1 Say who you are and where you are phoning from.
2 Say when your reservation is for and for how long.
3 Ask if you can come two weeks later.
4 !

Your teacher will play the part of the receptionist and will speak first.

(Adapted from AQA/NEAB – 1998)

Pour faire du camping …

Vous avez de la place pour une tente (une caravane)?
Nous sommes deux adultes et deux enfants.
Avez-vous un emplacement à l'ombre (près des douches)?
C'est combien par personne et par jour?
Est-ce que l'eau est potable?

To go camping …

Do you have room for a tent (a caravan)?
It's for two adults and two children.
Have you got a place in the shade (near the showers)?
How much is it per person per day?
Can you drink the water?

Pour aller à l'auberge de jeunesse …

Vous avez de la place pour deux personnes?
C'est pour un garçon et une fille.
L'auberge ferme à quelle heure?
Je peux louer un sac de couchage?
Je n'ai pas besoin de draps.
Il y a une salle de jeux?

To go to the youth hostel …

Have you got room for two people?
It's for one boy and one girl.
At what time does the hostel close?
Can I hire a sleeping bag?
I don't need sheets.
Is there a games room?

Pour louer un appartement …

Je voudrais louer un appartement du 30 juillet au 7 août.
L'appartement a combien de chambres?
La cuisine est équipée?
Y a-t-il des draps et des serviettes?

To rent a flat …

I'd like to rent a flat from 30th July to 7th August.
How many bedrooms does the flat have?
Is the kitchen equipped?
Are there sheets and towels?

Pour résoudre des problèmes …

Qu'est-ce qui ne va pas?
Il n'y a pas d'eau chaude.
La télévision (Le chauffage) ne marche pas.
Je voudrais une autre chambre.
Je ne dors pas à cause du bruit.
Il faut que je change de chambre aujourd'hui.
Nous n'avons plus de chambres.
Nous allions arriver à dix-huit heures.
J'arriverai en retard.
Mon avion a eu un retard d'une heure.
Il y a eu un accident sur l'autoroute.
Nous pourrons dîner en arrivant?
Je devrais arriver vers vingt et une heures.

To solve problems …

What's wrong?
There is no hot water.
The TV (The heating) isn't working.
I'd like another room.
I can't sleep because of the noise.
I must change rooms today.
We have no rooms left.
We were going to arrive at 6 p.m.
I will arrive late.
My plane was an hour late.
There was an accident on the motorway.
Will we be able to have dinner when we arrive?
I should arrive at about 9 p.m.

Vous venez d'arriver dans un hôtel à Cherbourg mais il y a un problème avec votre chambre. Vous voulez changer de chambre <u>aujourd'hui</u> et vous allez voir le directeur.

(Adapted from AQA/NEAB – 1998)

1 Act this conversation with a partner and learn the client's lines.

2 Partner A reads the manager's lines. Partner B covers the cartoon and uses these cues to act the part of the client:

• Problème.   • Détails du problème.   • Votre solution.   • Vous acceptez.

Exam Practice

A

1 Check that you know all the phrases on pages 66 and 68.
2 Cover the teacher's questions on the right and prepare your role in five minutes.
3 Look at the teacher's questions, which are in random order, and write the conversation in full.

Candidate's Role

You have reserved a place on a campsite in France. You phone to change your reservation.

1 Qui et d'où.
2 Raison.
3 Détails.
4 Changements.
5 Pourquoi.

a Alors, que voulez-vous faire?
b Vous pouvez me dire pourquoi?
c Allô, Camping Municipal?
d Ça s'écrit comment?
e Et que puis-je faire pour vous aider?
f Et quand voulez-vous venir?
g Vous avez réservé pour quelles dates?
h Et vous êtes combien?

B

1 Cover the Teacher's Role and prepare your role in five minutes.
2 Look at the Teacher's Role and practise the dialogue with a partner.

Teacher's Role

1 Allô, oui? *(Candidate's task: to say why he/she is phoning.)*
2 Quand voulez-vous venir exactement? *(Candidate's task: to respond, giving dates.)*
3 D'accord. Et que voulez-vous exactement? *(Candidate's task: to make the booking, giving number of people and other requirements.)*
4 Et qu'est-ce que vous allez faire pendant votre séjour? *(Candidate's task: to say what he/she intends to do.)*
5 Bonne idée!

Candidate's Role

Your family wants to rent a flat in France during the school summer holidays. You phone the owner to make the booking.
1 Téléphoner – pourquoi.
2 Dates.
3 Détails de la réservation.
4 !

Your teacher will play the part of the owner and will speak first.

(Adapted from AQA/NEAB – 1998)

3 Read the answers on the right given by one candidate. Mark each answer out of four. Then re-write the answers so that they all score the full four marks.

1 Je voudrais réserver un appartement.
2 Du 30 juillet au 30 août.
3 Je voudrais réserver l'appartement.
4 Je vais faire des excursions.

C

1 Cover the Teacher's Role and prepare your role in five minutes.
2 Practise the dialogue with a partner. Aim to score four marks for every response.

Teacher's Role

1 Allô, Hôtel Ibis. *(Candidate's task: to say he/she is going to be late.)*
2 Qu'est-ce qui s'est passé? *(Candidate's task: to give a reason for the delay.)*
3 Ça va, il n'y a pas de problème. *(Candidate's task: to ask if he/she can have a meal when he/she arrives.)*
4 Bien sûr. C'est à quel nom et ça s'écrit comment? *(Candidate's task: to give surname and spell it.)*
5 Et quand pensez-vous arriver? *(Candidate's task: to say when he/she expects to arrive.)*
6 D'accord, je parlerai au chef.

Candidate's Role

You have been delayed on your way to your hotel in France. You telephone to make arrangements for a meal.
1 Retard.
2 Raison.
3 Repas?
4 !

Your teacher will play the part of the receptionist and will speak first.

(AQA/NEAB – 1998)

These two pages contain role-play tests which have been set at GCSE. Practise them using the following guidelines until you find them easy: this is an excellent way to prepare for your own Speaking Test.

1 Revise the useful phrases as suggested.
2 Cover the Teacher's Role and prepare the Candidate's Role in three minutes.
3 Look at the Teacher's Role and, with a partner, practise the role-play.

> ### Exam Tip
> • Read the instructions carefully and prepare exactly what they say.
> • Decide whether you will use *tu* or *vous*.
> • Take care to pronounce your verbs correctly, e.g. do not pronounce the *e* when you say *j'aime* or the *es* when you say *tu aimes*.
> • If you have to say that **you want to** or **you would like**, use *je voudrais*. If you have to say that **you like** something, use *j'aime*.
> • Use the French that you know and keep it short and simple.

A

To prepare for this role-play, revise page 30.

Teacher's Role	Candidate's Role
Nous sommes au centre de loisirs. Moi, je suis l'employé(e). 1 Oui, monsieur (mademoiselle)? 2 Vous êtes combien? 3 Oui, monsieur (mademoiselle). 4 Ça fait cinquante francs. 5 A vingt heures trente.	You are at a leisure centre in France. 1 You want to play volleyball. 2 There are two adults and four children. 3 Ask how much it costs. 4 Ask what time the leisure centre closes. Your teacher will play the part of the receptionist and will speak first.

(AQA/NEAB – 1998)

B

To prepare for this role-play, revise pages 30 and 34.

Teacher's Role	Candidate's Role
Nous sommes chez toi. Tu parles avec ton ami(e). Moi, je suis ton ami(e). 1 Salut! 2 Oui. 3 Bonne idée. A quelle heure? 4 C'est combien? 5 Ce n'est pas trop cher.	Your French friend is staying at your house in Britain. 1 Ask if your friend likes films. 2 You would like to go to the cinema. 3 It starts at 8 o'clock. 4 It costs £4. Your teacher will play the part of your friend and will speak first.

(AQA/NEAB – 1998)

C

To prepare for this role play, revise pages 12, 22, 50 and 66.

Teacher's Role	Candidate's Role
Vous téléphonez à un restaurant en France. Moi, je suis le/la réceptionniste. 1 Bonsoir, monsieur (mademoiselle). 2 D'accord, monsieur (mademoiselle). 3 Pour quelle heure? 4 D'accord, monsieur (mademoiselle). 5 Oui, derrière le restaurant.	You are on holiday in France and you decide to telephone to book a meal in a restaurant. 1 You want to book for this evening. 2 You want a table for four. 3 You would like the table for 7.30 p.m. 4 Ask if there is a car park at the restaurant. Your teacher will play the part of the receptionist and will speak first.

(AQA/NEAB – 1998)

D

To prepare for this role-play, revise pages 12, 14 and 30.

Teacher's Role	**Candidate's Role**
Tu es chez ton ami(e), en France. Moi, je suis ton ami(e). 1 Ta maison est grande? 2 Comment est ta chambre? 3 Qu'est-ce qu'il y a, dans ta chambre? 4 C'est bien. 5 Je n'ai pas de télé dans ma chambre.	You are staying with your French friend, in France. You are talking about your home. 1 There are eight rooms in your house. 2 Your bedroom is quite small. 3 There is a wardrobe and a table. 4 Ask if your friend watches television in his/her bedroom. Your teacher will play the part of your friend and will speak first.

(AQA/NEAB – 1998)

E

To prepare for this role-play, revise pages 26 and 46.

Teacher's Role	**Candidate's Role**
Vous êtes dans un grand magasin à Cherbourg. Moi, je suis le vendeur/la vendeuse. 1 Bonjour. Je peux vous aider? 2 De quelle couleur? 3 Très bien. Vous aimez ce pull-over? 4 Quatre cents francs. 5 Je regrette, mais je n'ai rien à ce prix-là.	You are in a department store in Cherbourg. 1 You want to buy a jumper. 2 You want a black and white one. 3 Ask how much it is. 4 Say you only have 200 francs. Your teacher will play the part of the shop assistant and will speak first.

(Adapted from AQA/NEAB – 1998)

F

To prepare for this role-play, revise pages 30, 38 and 42.

Teacher's Role	**Candidate's Role**
Vous êtes au syndicat d'initiative, à Dieppe. Moi, je suis le/la réceptionniste. 1 Bonjour. Vous désirez? 2 Alors, elle est sur la Place Saint Pierre. 3 Non, elle est à dix minutes à pied. 4 A huit heures. 5 De rien. Au revoir.	You are in the tourist office in Dieppe. 1 Ask where the cathedral is. 2 Ask if it is far away. 3 Ask when it opens. 4 Say thank you and goodbye. Your teacher will play the part of the receptionist and will speak first.

(Adapted from AQA/NEAB – 1998)

G

To prepare for this role-play, revise pages 30, 34 and 54.

Teacher's Role	**Candidate's Role**
Tu es chez ton ami(e), en France. Moi, je suis ton ami(e). 1 Alors, qu'est-ce que tu vas faire, aujourd'hui? 2 Ah, très bien. 3 Il est en face de la maison. 4 A dix heures et demie. 5 Non, merci, je ne peux pas, ce matin.	You are staying with your friend in France. 1 You want to go to the swimming pool. 2 Ask where the bus stop is. 3 Ask what time the bus leaves. 4 Ask if your friend wants to go too. Your teacher will play the part of your friend and will speak first.

(Adapted from AQA/NEAB – 1998)

Practice these role-plays, on your own and with a partner, until you are word perfect. All these role-plays have been set at GCSE.

1 Revise the phrases on the pages suggested.

2 Cover the Teacher's Role and prepare the Candidate's Role in four minutes.

3 Look at the Teacher's Role and, with a partner, practise the role-play.

A

To prepare for this role-play, revise pages 26, 30 and 58.

Teacher's Role	Candidate's Role
1 Tu as une grande famille?	You have met a French boy/girl at the disco.
2 Tu peux me décrire ton frère?	1 Tell him/her you have a brother and two sisters.
3 Et qu'est-ce qu'il fait dans la vie?	2 Describe your brother's hair and eyes.
4 Et quels sont les passe-temps préférés de ton frère?	3 Tell him/her what your brother does for a living.
5 Alors, moi j'aime faire de l'équitation.	4 !
	When you see this – ! – you will have to respond to something which you have not prepared.
	Your teacher will play the part of the French boy/girl and will speak first.

(AQA/NEAB – 1998)

B

To prepare for this role-play, revise pages 12, 30 and 58.

Teacher's Role	Candidate's Role
1 Tu as un job?	You are talking to your French friend about your part-time job.
2 Tu prépares les repas?	1 Tell him/her you work in the kitchen of a restaurant.
3 C'est bien payé?	2 Tell him/her you do the washing up.
4 Que fais-tu avec l'argent que tu gagnes?	3 Tell him/her you earn £3 an hour.
5 Ah, c'est intéressant, ça.	4 !
	When you see this – ! – you will have to respond to something which you have not prepared.
	Your teacher will play the part of your friend and will speak first.

(AQA/NEAB – 1998)

C

To prepare for this role-play, revise pages 26, 34 and 46.

Teacher's Role	Candidate's Role
1 Tu veux aller en discothèque?	Your French friend asks if you want to go to the disco.
2 Comment s'appelle ton ami(e) et ça s'écrit comment?	1 Tell him/her you would like to invite a friend.
3 D'accord, ton ami(e) peut venir.	2 !
4 Qu'est-ce que tu vas porter?	3 Suggest where and when you will meet.
5 Moi, je vais porter un jean et une chemise.	4 Tell him/her what you will wear.
	When you see this – ! – you will have to respond to something which you have not prepared.
	Your teacher will play the part of your friend and will speak first.

(AQA/NEAB – 1998)

D

To prepare for this role-play, revise page 18.

Teacher's Role	Candidate's Role
1 Ça ne va pas? 2 Où as-tu mal? 3 Ah, quel dommage! 4 Bien sûr. Les voilà. Tu as besoin d'autre chose? 5 Bien sûr.	You are staying with your French friend. 1 You don't feel well. 2 ! 3 Ask if your friend has any aspirin. 4 Ask for some water. When you see this – ! – you will have to respond to something which you have not prepared. Your teacher will play the part of your friend.

(Adapted from AQA/NEAB – 1998)

E

To prepare for this role-play, revise pages 8 and 30.

Teacher's Role	Candidate's Role
1 Comment c'est pour toi, une journée au collège? 2 Quelle est ta matière préférée, et pourquoi? 3 Qu'est-ce que tu n'aimes pas, et pourquoi? 4 Et que fais-tu le soir, après l'école? 5 Moi, j'ai beaucoup de devoirs tous les soirs.	Your French friend asks you about your school. 1 Say what time your school starts and finishes. 2 Say which is your favourite subject and why. 3 Say which subject you don't like and why. 4 ! When you see this – ! – you will have to respond to something which you have not prepared. Your teacher will play the part of your friend.

(Adapted from AQA/NEAB – 1998)

F

To prepare for this role-play, revise pages 12, 14, 30 and 38.

Teacher's Role	Candidate's Role
1 Où habites-tu? 2 Elle est comment, ta maison? 3 Que fais-tu pour aider à la maison? 4 Moi aussi. Et que fais-tu pour t'amuser? 5 Ah, c'est intéressant, ça.	Your French friend asks about where you live. 1 Tell your friend that you live on the outskirts of town. 2 Say that your house is quite big with four bedrooms. 3 Say that you make your bed and do the vacuuming. 4 ! When you see this – ! – you will have to respond to something which you have not prepared. Your teacher will play the part of your friend and will speak first.

(AQA/NEAB – 1998)

G

To prepare for this role-play, revise pages 38 and 62.

Teacher's Role	Candidate's Role
1 Salut! Quel plaisir de te revoir! 2 J'ai été à la montagne avec des amis. 3 Il a fait assez beau. 4 On a fait une promenade. Tu préfères quelle sorte de vacances et pourquoi? 5 Ah, oui, c'est intéressant, ça.	You are talking to your French friend about holidays. 1 Ask where your friend went last year. 2 Ask what the weather was like. 3 Ask what your friend did in the evenings. 4 ! When you see this – ! – you will have to respond to something which you have not prepared. Your teacher will play the part of your friend and will speak first.

(Adapted from AQA/NEAB – 1998)

Here are some role-plays which have been set at Higher Tier at GCSE. Practise them using the guidelines below until you feel confident that you could cope with a role-play like this in your exam.

1 Revise the phrases on the pages suggested before each role-play.

2 Cover the Teacher's Role and prepare the Candidate's Role in four minutes.

3 Look at the Teacher's Role and, with a partner, practise the role-play.

Read carefully the notes in brackets in the Teacher's Role. These show you what you need to do to score full marks.

Exam Tips

• Read the instructions carefully. Sometimes, important instructions are given in the English introduction. Make sure that you include these details in your answers.

• To score the full four marks for each task, you must complete each one in detail. Remember that it is not easy to predict exactly what you have to say, so you must be flexible enough to answer the question your teacher asks even if it is not the question you prepared. Listen very carefully to what your teacher says.

• When you are asked to describe something, give at least two details.

• When you are asked to make a suggestion or express an opinion, always follow it with a reason.

• Be prepared to negotiate. If you are planning an activity, always be prepared to suggest an alternative activity or another time or place.

• Be prepared to spell your name and address and to give your telephone number, including the dialling code.

• Be prepared for a mixture of topics. Examiners often combine more than one topic in a role-play.

• Keep your answers detailed but simple. Use French you know.

A

To prepare for this role-play, revise pages 8 and 10, 14 and 16, 26 and 28, 50 and 52.

Teacher's Role

1 Allô, oui. *(Candidate's task: to apologise for not writing and give a reason.)*

2 Comment est-ce que tu t'entends avec ta sœur? *(Candidate's task: to say whether he/she gets on with his/her sister.)*

3 Elle est comment, ta sœur? *(Candidate's task: to give two details about his/her sister's personality.)*

4 J'aimerais bien lui trouver une correspondante. Tu penses qu'elle aimerait ça? *(Candidate's task: to say whether his/her sister would like a penfriend and why.)*

Candidate's Role

You telephone your French friend to apologise for not writing and he/she asks about your sister.

1 Excuses et raison.

3 Sœur: relations.

4 Sœur: personnalité.

5 !

Your teacher will play the part of your friend and will speak first.

(AQA/NEAB – 1998)

B

To prepare for this role-play, revise pages 26 and 28, 34 and 36, 46 and 48, 50 and 52, 54 and 56.

Teacher's Role

1 Oui, je peux vous aider? *(Candidate's task: to say that he/she can't find his/her French friend.)*

2 Où aviez-vous rendez-vous dans la gare et à quelle heure? *(Candidate's task: to say when and where they had arranged to meet.)*

3 Et que porte votre ami(e)? *(Candidate's task: to describe the clothes of the French friend, giving three details.)*

4 Pouvez-vous décrire votre ami(e)? *(Candidate's task: to say what the French friend looks like, giving three details.)*

5 Ah, voilà votre ami(e) qui arrive.

Candidate's Role

You arrive at a station in France and find that your French friend is not there to meet you. You go to the Information Desk.

1 Problème.

2 Où et quand.

3 Vêtements.

4 !

Your teacher will play the part of the clerk and will speak first.

(AQA/NEAB – 1998)

C

To prepare for this role-play, revise pages 18 and 20, 38 and 40, 42, 54 and 56.

Teacher's Role	Candidate's Role

Teacher's Role

1 Allô, oui. Je peux vous aider?
  (Candidate's task: to say he/she wants to make an appointment.)

2 Alors, qu'est-ce qui ne va pas?
  (Candidate's task: to explain his/her symptoms.)

3 Le médecin pourra vous voir lundi prochain.
  (Candidate's task: to point out that it is urgent and that the advertisement offers immediate appointments.)

4 Où êtes-vous? Et il vous faut combien de temps pour venir à la clinique?
  (Candidate's task: to say where he/she is and how long it will take him/her to get to the clinic.)

5 Alors, venez tout de suite.

Candidate's Role

You are taken ill whilst on holiday in France. You ring the doctor to make an urgent appointment for today.

> ## Centre d'urgences médicales
> Appelez-nous et nous vous
> verrons tout de suite.
> ☎ 04 67 94 01
> *Clinique Puginier*
> *268 route de Douvres*

1 Raison de l'appel.
2 Symptômes.
3 Rendez-vous.
4 !

Your teacher will play the part of the doctor's receptionist and will speak first.

(Adapted from AQA/NEAB – 1998)

D

To prepare for this role-play, revise pages 30 and 32, 34 and 36, 38 and 40, 54 and 56.

Teacher's Role

1 Où se trouve Supaland exactement?
  (Candidate's task: to say where Supaland is.)

2 Qu'est-ce qu'il y a à faire? *(Candidate's task: to explain what there is to do there, giving two details.)*

3 Super! On y va quand et comment?
  (Candidate's task: to suggest when and how to travel.)

4 D'accord, mais j'ai très peu d'argent. Je voudrais vraiment y aller mais qu'est-ce que je peux faire? Tu as une idée, toi?
  (Candidate's task: to suggest a solution to the problem.)

5 Bonne idée!

Candidate's Role

Your French friend is staying with you. You are very enthusiastic about going to this theme park, but your friend isn't sure.

1 Où se trouve Supaland.
2 Activités.
3 Détails du voyage.
4 !

Your teacher will play the part of your friend and will speak first.

(Adapted from AQA/NEAB – 1998)

E

To prepare for this role-play, revise pages 44, 50 and 52, 54 and 56, 66 and 68.

Teacher's Role

1 Allô, je peux vous aider?
  (Candidate's task: to explain what the problem is.)

2 Quel dommage. Qu'est-ce qui ne va pas exactement?
  (Candidate's task: to explain exactly what's wrong.)

3 Ah, oui, c'est peut-être grave. Où êtes-vous exactement?
  (Candidate's task: to explain exactly where the car is.)

4 Alors, nous fermons dans deux heures. Qu'est-ce que vous allez faire?
  (Candidate's task: to say what he/she is going to do.)

5 D'accord.

Candidate's Role

You have almost reached Cherbourg to catch a ferry when the car in which you are travelling breaks down. You need help urgently so you phone a garage.

1 Problème.
2 Détails du problème.
3 Où.
4 !

Your teacher will play the part of the garage owner and will speak first.

(Adapted from AQA/NEAB – 1998)

Numbers & Dates

Les numéros

1	*un*	11	*onze*	21	*vingt et un*	91	*quatre-vingt-onze*
2	*deux*	12	*douze*	22	*vingt-deux*	100	*cent*
3	*trois*	13	*treize*	30	*trente*	101	*cent un*
4	*quatre*	14	*quatorze*	40	*quarante*	102	*cent deux*
5	*cinq*	15	*quinze*	50	*cinquante*	200	*deux cents*
6	*six*	16	*seize*	60	*soixante*	201	*deux cent un*
7	*sept*	17	*dix-sept*	70	*soixante-dix*	1 000	*mille*
8	*huit*	18	*dix-huit*	80	*quatre-vingts*	1 000 000	*un million*
9	*neuf*	19	*dix-neuf*	81	*quatre-vingt-un*		
10	*dix*	20	*vingt*	90	*quatre-vingt-dix*		

1st	*premier, première*	6th	*sixième*
2nd	*deuxième*	7th	*septième*
3rd	*troisième*	8th	*huitième*
4th	*quatrième*	9th	*neuvième*
5th	*cinquième*	10th	*dixième*

Quelle heure est-il?

Il est une heure.	It's one o'clock.
Il est deux (trois) heures.	It's two (three) o'clock.
Il est quatorze heures.	It's 14.00 (2 p.m.).
A vingt heures dix.	At 20.10 (8.10 p.m.).
A onze heures et quart.	At 11.15.
A midi et demi.	At 12.30 p.m.
A minuit.	At midnight.
A sept heures moins cinq.	At five to seven.

Les dates

Les jours		**Les mois**	
lundi	Monday	*janvier*	January
mardi	Tuesday	*février*	February
mercredi	Wednesday	*mars*	March
jeudi	Thursday	*avril*	April
vendredi	Friday	*mai*	May
samedi	Saturday	*juin*	June
dimanche	Sunday	*juillet*	July
		août	August
		septembre	September
		octobre	October
		novembre	November
		décembre	December

Mon anniversaire, c'est le premier février.	My birthday is on the 1st of February.
Aujourd'hui, c'est le onze avril.	Today is the 11th of April.
Nous partons le vingt et un août.	We leave on the 21st of August.
Du dix-neuf juin jusqu'au deux juillet.	From the 19th of June until the 2nd of July.

Glossaire *Glossary*

This is a list of some important French words which appear in the book.

A

un accident *accident*
une activité *activity*
une addition *bill*
une agence *agency*
aider *to help*
alcool *alcohol*
allô *hello (on telephone)*
une alouette *swallow (bird)*
une ambiance *atmosphere*
un(e) ami(e) *friend*
une année *year*
août *August*
un appel *call*
appeler *to call*
après *after*
argent *money*
attendre *to wait (for)*
j'aurai (avoir) *I will have*
autre *other*
avant *before*

B

bientôt *soon*
bienvenue *welcome*
britannique *British*
un bureau de change *money exchange office*
un bureau des objets trouvés *lost property office*

C

un camping *campsite*
ce qui ne va pas *what's wrong*
une chambre *room*
la chance *luck*
(bonne chance) *(good luck)*
un changement *change*
changer *to change*
un chef *boss; chef*
chez *at the home of*
une clinique *private hospital*
comment *how*
comprendre *to understand*
la connaissance *knowledge; acquaintance*
(faire la connaissance) *(to get to know)*
le contenu *contents*
un(e) correspondant(e) *penfriend*
la Côte d'Azur *French Riviera*
une couleur *colour*
un(e) cousin(e) *cousin*
coûter *to cost*

D

d'accord *agreed, OK*
une date *date*
décider de *to decide to*
décrire *to describe*
dedans *inside*
une description *description*
désirer *to like*
un détail *detail*
difficile *difficult*
un directeur *manager*
dommage *shame*

(quel dommage) *(what a shame)*
dormir *to sleep*
d'où *where from*
Douvres *Dover*

E

un échange *exchange*
l'Ecosse *Scotland*
écouter *to listen*
un écran *screen*
un élève *pupil*
un emploi *job*
une émission *programme*
une enquête *survey*
ensuite *then, after that*
un enterrement *funeral*
entre *between*
une entrée *entrance*
environ *about*
équitation *horse riding*
éviter *to avoid*
une excuse *excuse, apology*
une expérience *experience*
expliquer *to explain*

F

faire les magasins *to go shopping*
je fasse (faire) *I should do*
il faudrait *it would be necessary*
fermer *to close*
fêter *to celebrate*
la fin *end*
fort *strong; good at*
un frein *brake*
un frère *brother*
le fromage *cheese*

G

une gare *station*

H

une heure *hour; time*
l'huile *oil*
huit jours *week*

I

immatriculation (numéro d') *registration number*
un infirmier *male nurse*
à l'intérieur *inside*

J

un(e) jeune *young person*
un jour *day*
une journée *day*
juillet *July*

L

un lac *lake*
une langue *language*
un lieu *place*
lundi *Monday*

M

malheureusement *unfortunately*
un marché *market*
une marque *make*
un mécanicien *mechanic*

un médecin *doctor*
meilleur *best*
mille *a thousand*
mixte *mixed*
moins (de) *less (than)*
un moment *moment, time*
un moniteur *instructor; supervisor* (une monitrice)
une montagne *mountain*
le monde *world; people*
(beaucoup de monde) *(a lot of people)*
mort *dead*
un moyen *means*

N

ni … ni … *neither … nor …*
nouveau, nouvelle *new*
(vos) nouvelles *(your) news*
un numéro *number*

O

un objet *object, thing*
une opinion *opinion*
un ordinateur *computer*
où *where*
où aller *where to go*

P

un palais des congrès *conference centre*
parfois *sometimes*
un parking *car park*
à part *apart from, except for*
un(e) partenaire *partner*
pas trop *not too much*
se passer *to happen*
pendant *during*
pendant que *while*
penser *to think*
peu *little*
peut-être *perhaps*
un pique-nique *picnic*
une place *square (in town)*
un plaisir *pleasure*
une plage *beach*
un plat *dish; food*
il pleut *it is raining*
plus *more*
une poire *pear*
polyvalent *comprehensive*
un(e) pompiste *petrol pump attendant*
porter *to wear*
poser *to ask; to put*
poster *to post*
pour cent *percent*
pourquoi *why*
pourra (pouvoir) *will be able*
préféré *favourite*
prenons (prendre) *let's have; let's take*
un prix *price; prize*
un problème *problem*
prochain *next*
prouver *to prove*

Q

quand *when*
quelque chose *something*

Glossaire Glossary

R
une raison   *reason*
un reçu   *receipt*
relations   *relationship*
un rendez-vous   *meeting; appointment; date*
renseignements   *information*
rentrer   *to return, to go back (home)*
un repas   *meal*
répondre   *to reply, to answer*
une réponse   *answer*
une réservation   *reservation, booking*
un retard   *delay*
un retour   *return*
revoir   *to see again*
la rivalité   *rivalry*

S
un sac   *bag*
un salaire   *salary*
salut   *hello, hi*
satisfait   *satisfied*
un séjour   *stay*
(faire un séjour)   *(to stay)*
se sentir (malade)   *to feel (ill)*
un serveur   *waiter*
une serveuse   *waitress*
servir   *to serve*
seul   *the only one; alone*

seulement   *only*
si   *if; yes*
une sœur   *sister*
soigner   *to look after; to take care of*
une solution   *solution*
une sorte de   *sort of (concert, work)*
 (concert, travail)
soudain   *suddenly*
souvent   *often*
une suggestion   *suggestion*
la Suisse   *Switzerland*
suisse   *Swiss*
un supplément   *supplement, extra charge*
une surprise-partie   *party*
les symptômes   *symptoms, what's wrong*

T
le tabac   *tobacco; tobacconist's shop*
le TGV   *high speed train*
 (Train à Grande Vitesse)
un théâtre   *theatre*
tomber   *to fall*
tomber en panne   *to break down*
tous les deux   *both*
tout   *everything*
(C'est tout?)   *(Is that all?)*
tout de suite   *straight away, immediately*

trouver   *to find*
se trouve   *is*

U
un uniforme   *uniform*

V
en vacances   *on holiday*
un vélo   *bike*
un vendeur   *shop assistant*
 (une vendeuse)
le vendredi   *Friday*
venir de   *to have just*
 (done something)
verrons (voir)   *will see*
les vêtements   *clothes*
une vie   *life*
(faire dans la vie)   *(to do for a living)*
vivre   *to live*
voilà   *there is, there are*
votre   *your*
une voiture   *car*
un voyage   *journey*
vraiment   *really*
vu (voir)   *seen*

Y
y   *there*

English–French Anglais–Français

A
abroad   *à l'étranger*
accent   *un accent*
to accept   *accepter*
actor   *un acteur*
actress   *une actrice*
to adore   *adorer*
advertisement   *une annonce*
after   *après*
Africa   *l'Afrique*
again   *encore une fois*
against   *contre*
air hostess   *une hôtesse de l'air*
airmail   *par avion*
A-level   *le bac(calauréat)*
always   *toujours*
anorak   *un anorak*
to answer   *répondre*
answering machine   *un répondeur*
 (téléphonique)
an arm   *un bras*
armchair   *un fauteuil*
to arrive   *arriver*
at least   *au moins*
aunt   *une tante*
Austria   *l'Autriche*

B
baby   *un bébé*
badminton   *le badminton*
a bag   *un sac*
baker   *un boulanger, une boulangère*
balcony   *un balcon*
beautiful   *beau (belle)*
because   *parce que*

bed   *un lit*
(to make the bed)   *(faire le lit)*
beef   *le bœuf*
beer   *la bière*
before   *avant*
beginning   *le début*
Belgian   *belge*
Belgium   *la Belgique*
best   *meilleur*
between   *entre*
bicycle   *une bicyclette*
biology   *la biologie*
bird   *un oiseau*
biro   *un bic*
biscuit   *un biscuit*
blond   *blond*
a book   *un livre*
a boss   *un patron, un chef*
a bowl   *un bol*
boy   *un garçon*
broken down   *en panne*
brown   *marron, brun*
building   *un bâtiment*
bus   *un bus, un autobus*
butcher   *un boucher, une bouchère*
to buy   *acheter*

C
cabbage   *le chou*
to camp   *faire du camping*
cake shop   *une pâtisserie*
calm   *calme*
car   *une voiture*
caravan   *une caravane*

carpet   *une moquette*
carrot   *une carotte*
cartoon   *un dessin animé; une bande dessinée*
 (une BD)
cashier   *un caissier, une caissière*
cassette recorder   *un magnétophone à*
 cassettes
cathedral   *une cathédrale*
cauliflower   *le chou-fleur*
cereals   *les céréales*
charming   *charmant*
cheap   *bon marché*
chemistry   *la chimie*
chemist's shop   *une pharmacie*
cherry   *une cerise*
classical   *classique*
to clear the table   *débarrasser la table*
a cloud   *un nuage*
a coach   *un autocar, un car*
coast   *la côte*
a coat   *un manteau*
coca-cola   *le coca(-cola)*
a cold   *un rhume*
to collect   *collectionner*
a colour   *une couleur*
computer   *un ordinateur*
computer   *un(e) informaticien(ne)*
 programmer
cooker   *une cuisinière*
corner   *un coin*
to correct   *corriger*
country   *un pays*
countryside   *la campagne*
cow   *une vache*

Glossaire Glossary

crisps   *les chips*
a cup   *une tasse*
cupboard   *un placard*

D
dad   *papa*
dangerous   *dangereux(euse)*
dark (colour)   *foncé*
daughter   *une fille*
dentist   *un dentiste*
to depend   *dépendre*
(that depends)   *(ça dépend)*
a deposit   *les arrhes*
dessert   *un dessert*
documentary   *un documentaire*
door   *une porte*
to draw   *dessiner*
dry   *sec (sèche)*
dustbin   *une poubelle*

E
easy   *facile*
egg   *un œuf*
(boiled egg)   *(un œuf à la coque)*
electric   *électrique*
e-mail   *le courrier électronique*
empty   *vide*
entrance   *une entrée*
Europe   *l'Europe*
everybody   *tout le monde*
example   *un exemple*
except   *sauf*
exchange   *un échange*
exercise book   *un cahier*
an exit   *une sortie*
to explain   *expliquer*
eye   *un œil (les yeux)*

F
famous   *célèbre*
fashion   *la mode*
favourite   *préféré*
a field   *un champ*
to fill   *remplir*
a finger   *un doigt*
a fish   *un poisson*
a flower   *une fleur*
fog   *le brouillard*
a fork   *une fourchette*
fortunately   *heureusement*
free   *gratuit; libre*
to freeze   *geler*
freezer   *un congélateur*
Friday   *le vendredi*
friend   *un(e) ami(e)*
(school friend)   *(un(e) camarade de classe)*
fruit   *un fruit*
fruit juice   *un jus de fruit*
full   *plein*
funny   *amusant*

G
game   *un jeu*
Germany   *l'Allemagne*
to get up   *se lever*
ginger (hair)   *(les cheveux) roux*
girl   *une fille*
glass   *le verre*
to go   *aller*

to go home   *rentrer*
to play golf   *jouer au golf*
grandfather   *un grand-père*
grandmother   *une grand-mère*
grandparent   *un grand-parent*
grapefruit   *un pamplemousse*
Greece   *la Grèce*
Greek   *grec (grecque)*
grey   *gris*
grocer   *un épicier, une épicière*
a group   *un groupe*

H
half brother   *un demi-frère*
half sister   *une demi-sœur*
hamburger   *un hamburger*
handball   *le handball*
happy   *heureux(euse)*
happy Christmas   *joyeux Noël*
hat   *un chapeau*
to hate   *détester*
to hear   *entendre*
heard   *entendu*
heart   *un cœur*
heavy   *lourd*
to hire   *louer*
hockey   *le hockey*
Holland   *la Hollande*
honey   *le miel*
hospital   *un hôpital*
hot chocolate   *le chocolat chaud*
to be hungry   *avoir faim*
husband   *un mari*

I
to imagine   *imaginer*
important   *important*
impossible   *impossible*
information office   *un bureau de renseignements*
inhabitant   *un habitant*
to be interested in   *s'intéresser à*
Ireland   *l'Irlande*
Irish   *irlandais*
Italy   *l'Italie*
Italian   *italien*

J
jacket   *une veste*
jazz   *le jazz*
jeans   *un jean*
job   *un métier; un job; un emploi*
jumper   *un pull-over*

K
kitchen   *une cuisine*
a knife   *un couteau*

L
laboratory   *un laboratoire*
lake   *un lac*
language   *une langue*
late   *en retard*
to laugh   *rire*
lawn   *une pelouse*
at least   *au moins*
left luggage office   *une consigne*
leg   *une jambe*
lemon   *un citron*
to lend   *prêter*

lesson   *une leçon, un cours*
light (colour)   *clair*
light (weight)   *léger (légère)*
a list   *une liste*
a little (more)   *un peu (plus)*
lorry   *un camion*
to lose   *perdre*
to love   *adorer*
love film   *un film d'amour*
luggage   *les bagages*

M
magazine   *un magazine*
market   *un marché*
meat   *la viande*
micro-wave oven   *un four à micro-ondes*
midday break   *la pause de midi*
milk   *le lait*
(coffee with milk)   *(un café-crème)*
(tea with milk)   *(un thé au lait)*
a million   *un million*
a mirror   *un miroir*
a mistake   *une erreur, une faute*
month   *un mois*
mountain   *une montagne*
mum   *maman*
museum   *un musée*

N
name   *un nom*
(first name)   *(un prénom)*
(surname)   *(un nom de famille)*
narrow   *étroit*
nasty   *méchant*
neck   *un cou*
to need to   *il faut*
new   *nouveau (nouvelle)*
New Year   *le Nouvel An*
nice (person)   *sympa, gentil*
noise   *un bruit*
nose   *un nez*
Northern Ireland   *l'Irlande du Nord*
a number   *un numéro*
nylon   *le nylon*

O
or   *ou*
ouch!   *aïe!*
outside   *dehors*
outskirts   *la banlieue*

P
pair of shorts   *un short*
paper   *le papier*
parcel   *un paquet*
a park   *un parc, un jardin public*
a party   *une surprise-partie, une boum*
passport   *un passeport*
pastry   *la pâtisserie*
pea   *un petit pois*
pear   *une poire*
pencil   *un crayon*
penfriend   *un(e) correspondant(e)*
pepper   *le poivre*
perhaps   *peut-être*
phone box   *une cabine téléphonique*
photo   *une photo*
physics   *la physique*
a piece   *un morceau*

Glossaire Glossary

pillow *un oreiller*
pineapple *un ananas*
a pitch *un terrain*
a place *un endroit, un lieu*
plane *un avion*
plate *une assiette*
to play cards *jouer aux cartes*
police officer *un agent de police*
police station *un commissariat*
polite *poli*
pop music *la musique pop*
Portugal *le Portugal*
postcode *un code postal*
postman *un facteur*
post office *une poste, un bureau de poste*
to prefer *préférer*
price *le prix*
problem *un problème*
to pull *tirer*
pupil *un(e) élève*
to push *pousser*
pyjamas *un pyjama*

Q

a question *une question*
quick *rapide, vite*

R

rain *la pluie*
to rain *pleuvoir (il pleut)*
to read *lire*
a record *un disque*
religious *religieux*
to rent *louer*
to repeat *répéter*
to reply *répondre*
a result *un résultat*
to return *revenir*
river *une rivière*
rock music *la musique rock*
rice *le riz*
rich *riche*
to be right *avoir raison*
room (in a house) *une pièce*
rug *un tapis*
rugby *le rugby*
a rule *une règle*
ruler *une règle*

S

sad *triste*
salad *une salade*
sale (in shop) *une solde*
salesperson (in shops) *un vendeur, une vendeuse*
Saturday *le samedi*
saucer *une soucoupe*
to save up *faire des économies*
school (rule) *(une règle) scolaire*
Scotland *l'Ecosse*
Scottish *écossais*

sea *la mer*
seafood *les fruits de mer*
selfish *égoïste*
settee *un canapé*
several *plusieurs*
to share *partager*
a shop *une boutique, un magasin*
shoe *une chaussure*
shy *timide*
to sing *chanter*
singer *un chanteur, une chanteuse*
skirt *une jupe*
to sleep *dormir*
slow *lent*
to smoke *fumer*
snow *la neige*
to snow *neiger*
soap *le savon*
sock *une chaussette*
sofa *un canapé*
sometimes *quelquefois, parfois*
son *un fils*
song *une chanson*
soon *bientôt*
Spain *l'Espagne*
spectacles *les lunettes*
squash *le squash*
steak *le steak, le bifteck*
a spoon *une cuiller, une cuillère*
stepbrother *un beau-frère*
stepfather *un beau-père*
stepmother *une belle-mère*
stepsister *une belle-sœur*
stomach *le ventre*
(to have stomach ache) *(avoir mal au ventre)*
to study *étudier*
sugar *le sucre*
sun *le soleil*
a sweet *un bonbon*
sweet shop *une confiserie*
swimming pool *une piscine*
swimsuit *un maillot de bain*
Swiss *suisse*
to switch on *allumer*
Switzerland *la Suisse*

T

taxi *un taxi*
a team *une équipe*
telephone box *une cabine téléphonique*
to thank *remercier*
thing *une chose*
to be thirsty *avoir soif*
a thousand *mille*
to tick *cocher*
to tidy my things *ranger mes affaires*
a tie *une cravate*
tights *un collant*
timetable *un horaire (trains, etc.); un emploi du temps (school)*

tin (of peaches) *une boîte (de pêches)*
toilet *un WC, les toilettes*
tourist office *un syndicat d'initiative, un office du tourisme*
transistor radio *un transistor*
to translate *traduire*
to travel *voyager*
travel agent's *une agence de voyages*
traveller's cheque *un chèque de voyage*
true *vrai*
a typist *une dactylo*

U

uncle *un oncle*
to underline *souligner*
understand *comprendre*
understood *compris*
unemployed *au chômage*
unemployed person *un chômeur*
unfortunately *malheureusement*
unhappy *malheureux(euse)*
USA *les Etats-Unis*
to use *utiliser*
useless *inutile*
usually *d'habitude*

V

veal *le veau*
vegetable *un légume*
video machine *un magnétoscope*
view *une vue*
vinegar *le vinaigre*
violet *violet*
volleyball *le volley*

W

to wait (for) *attendre*
waiter *un garçon de café, un serveur*
waitress *une serveuse*
wash basin *un lavabo*
washing machine *une machine à laver*
to wear *porter*
weak *faible*
weather forecast *la météo*
welcome *bienvenue*
Welsh *gallois*
wet *mouillé*
wife *une femme*
wind *le vent*
window *une fenêtre*
without *sans*
wood *le bois*
wool *la laine*
word *un mot*
to write *écrire*
wrong *faux (fausse)*
to be wrong *avoir tort*

Y

yellow *jaune*
youth hostel *une auberge de jeunesse*